HOLY MEN
and WOMEN *of the*
ORDER *of* MALTA

HOLY MEN
and WOMEN *of the*
ORDER *of* MALTA

THE CANONIZED
AND BEATIFIED
FROM THE 12TH
TO 21ST CENTURY

RICHARD J. WOLFF, KJ

TAN Books
Gastonia, North Carolina

Holy Men and Women of the Order of Malta: The Canonized and Beatified from the 12th to the 21st Century © 2021 Richard J. Wolff

Unless otherwise noted, Scripture quotations are from the Revised Standard Version of the Bible—Second Catholic Edition (Ignatius Edition), copyright © 2006 National Council of the Churches of Christ in the United States of America. Used by permission. All rights reserved.

Cover design by Caroline Green

Library of Congress Control Number: 2021939990
ISBN: 978-1-5051-2124-7
Kindle ISBN: 978-1-5051-2125-4
ePUB ISBN: 978-1-5051-2126-1

Published in the United States by
TAN Books
PO Box 269
Gastonia, NC 28053
www.TANBooks.com

Printed in the United States of America

To "our lords, the poor and the sick," for whom the Order of Malta has toiled for over nine hundred years

"We have to become saints. We have to become like Christ. Anything less is simply not enough."

—Anne Rice (in the Catholic phase of her spiritual journey)

Contents

Foreword

Amonograph on the lives of the Order of Malta's saints, which applies historical analysis, is long overdue. The order's saints, especially its medieval crop, have suffered far too long from the syrupy pens of well-intentioned, but misguided, hagiographers. In the following pages, the reader will find a refreshingly balanced view of the lives of these holy men and women and a serious attempt to separate fact from fiction.

Much of what the reader will encounter in this book on the order's saints underscores the existential peculiarity of the Order of Malta: its uniqueness as a religious order, with a military mission, a focus on active ministry to the sick and poor, and an emphasis on nobiliary traditions. All of this is bound up in a sovereign state recognized by the United Nations and over one hundred countries around the world. The Order of Malta, which has existed for one thousand years, is like no other religious order in the Church. Over centuries, it has adapted to a multiplicity of situations, often finding itself with its proverbial back to the wall, but somehow it always survived and often flourished.

Manuscript G 55 in the Morgan Library and Museum in New York tells us something about the order's peculiar nature. The manuscript is not the sort usually associated with a member of a religious order. Created in France in the mid-1460s, it is a book of hours. Popular in the Middle Ages, such books catered to the spiritual aspirations of the growing body of literate lay people who wished to pray as did the monks and nuns in their cloisters. Reflecting that desire, the calendars in these manuscripts follow the liturgical year, and in more luxurious volumes, there are miniatures that illustrate the saints and major feast days.

The latter is certainly the case with this carefully prepared manuscript. Fortunately, however, this volume went even one step further. It lets us deduce that at the very least its owner was neither a monk nor mendicant, and neither lay nor clerical. The owner's coat of arms decorates most folios, and three miniatures show him in knightly stances, clad in a black robe emblazoned with the distinctive cross of the Order of St. John. Finally, the miniature of a galley packed with Knights of Saint John prepared to do battle with a Turkish ship seals the identity of the person who had commissioned the manuscript. He was Pierre de Bosredont: a noble, a knight, and a religious of the Order of Saint John of Jerusalem—not exactly the average fifteenth-century (or any century for that matter) religious.

Without a doubt, the Order of St. John of Jerusalem has evolved over time, and the addition of "Rhodes and Malta" to the name is only the most obvious example. Through the centuries, the character of its membership has changed as well. Pierre de Bosredont, for instance, may have epitomized the best in its ranks in the fifteenth century, but he would have felt distinctly out of place when Pope Paschal II chartered the order in 1113. Conversely, knights in the style of de Bosredont had pretty much disappeared from the ranks of the order by the nineteenth century.

This is not to cast aspersions on de Bosredont or on any other knight of the order. Rather, historical circumstances forced the order to adapt or die. Its ability to change distinguishes it from the Order of the Temple and the many other orders that have long since gone extinct. Further, as the work of the order has changed, notions about its spiritual mission and expectations of holiness among its members have changed in tandem.

If work and spirituality impacted one another profoundly, we need to stress one other important point. Throughout its history, the activities of the Order of Saint John have differed rather dramatically from those of nearly every other order in the Church. If then the order encouraged holiness in its members, it was not the conventional holiness that one expected to find among Benedictine or Dominican saints. Put simply, no one expected to find contemplative ascetics in the Order of Saint John. And students would have been equally startled to hear a knight of Saint John lecturing on philosophy at the University of Paris.

The Order of St. John is one of the oldest orders in the Church. With roots that preceded by many years its recognition by Pope Paschal II, it was chartered to serve sick and poor pilgrims who found themselves stranded in the holy city of Jerusalem. Later, during the Crusades, it added to that mission a reputation for military prowess. Yet, perhaps because of that, it is not known for a roster of saints that might compare favorably with its peers in the Latin Christian world. It had no St. Benedict, no St. Francis or Claire or

Dominic, no Catherine of Siena or Ignatius Loyola. In fact, no medieval saintly figures in the order easily come to mind, save perhaps for Blessed Gerard, and his reputation scarcely reaches beyond members of the order.

Members of the Sovereign Military Hospitaller Order of St. John of Jerusalem of Rhodes and of Malta wear its history on their sleeves. The cross itself likely came from a colony of merchants from Amalfi. With the sanction of the Fatimid caliphs in Egypt, they had established a trading enclave in Jerusalem, and there they founded the Benedictine abbey of St. Mary of the Latins. The abbey in turn put in place a hospice to serve poor and sick pilgrims in Jerusalem next to the church of the nativity of St. John the Baptist. As the work of the hospice grew, it became difficult to reconcile the need to staff the hospital with the demands of claustral life. In time, the monks relinquished control of the hospice, and it became an independent entity under the direction of Frá Gerard. In 1113, that foundation became the home of the Order of St. John of Jerusalem.

From its origin, the order stood literally and figuratively on a new frontier. Spiritually, its very foundation depended on an ethos that was just starting to sprout in the Latin Christian world. Since the time of the Emperor Charlemagne in the early ninth century, the Rule of St. Benedict had been mandated as the sole guide for religious foundations in the empire. With the rule's emphasis on claustral life and the public recitation of the divine office, life in a Benedictine monastery was meant to be a full-time job. While each monastery did have a guesthouse, into which monks received all guests "as if they were Christ himself," only a small coterie of monks tended to the needs of the guests. Beyond that, monks were barred from public ministry, and that likely explains why the monks of St. Mary's gladly surrendered their hospice to Frá Gerard. It had become simply too much for them to handle.

The only rival to Benedict's rule was the much shorter Rule of Saint Augustine. It became the basis for orders of canons, who combined life in a cloister with pastoral service. But even they were not yet to the point at which the mendicants found themselves in the early thirteenth century. To the personal sanctification to which the monastic orders committed themselves, the mendicants added a second element. Service to the Church would be the complement to lives of personal holiness, and this led directly to the plethora of active orders that burst on the scene in the sixteenth century.

Compared with other medieval orders, the Order of St. John found itself in uncharted territory. It was not a monastic order, and it would not commit itself to life in a cloister. Nor was it an order that engaged in service that was exclusively pastoral or educational, as was the case with the mendicants. Service to the sick and the poor was at the core of the mission of the Order of St. John, but there had yet to be articulated a spirituality that would describe such a mission. No one should be surprised that from the very beginning, its spiritual ideals were a work in progress. They have been so ever since. Despite the novelty of marrying personal spiritual growth for the knights with service to the sick and the poor, it was still an idea whose time had come. That combination provided the framework for centuries of experiment and development.

More than anyone, it was Frá Gerard who shaped the ethos that has guided the Order of St. John through the centuries. Though we know little about his life, as explained in the following pages, we do know that he was something of an organizational genius. He governed the hospice in Jerusalem, coordinated a series of hostels that funneled pilgrims and financial support from Western Europe to the Holy Land, and formed a community that over time would accomplish far more than its numbers would warrant. All the while he would create a legacy of service that would inspire a steady flow of recruits to Jerusalem.

Frá Gerard's greatest imprint on the spirituality of the order was its Christocentric character. Acting on the teaching of Jesus that "what you do for the least of people you do for me," Gerard translated that into the order's mission to serve "our lords the sick and the poor." It was a double entendre that all would have understood at the time. Members should see the face of Our Lord Jesus Christ in the faces of the sick and the poor. But they would also see in the sick and the poor their personal lords. The sick and the poor had intrinsic value, despite being among the least in society.

A host of other sources reinforced this Christocentric work. Gerard need only recall that one of the first actions taken by the apostles after the ascension of Jesus was the appointment of deacons to see to the needs of widows and orphans. More immediately, the Benedictine view of hospitality was a value that Gerard likely knew well from his association with St. Mary of the Latins. "Receive all guests as Christ" easily transferred from the monastic guesthouse to the hospice. Finally, the Fatimid caliph who chartered the hospice did so on the condition that the brothers serve the sick and the poor of all faiths. If that seemed difficult for some to accept, it still reflects the Nicene Creed's statement that all are created in the image of God. That has been a constituent element of Christian and Hospitaller service from the beginning.

Much of Gerard's legacy was unwritten, but we can tease some of it from other evidence. The eight-pointed cross embodied the Beatitudes, for example. Another source, the Rule of Raymond du Puy, certainly reflects the values of Gerard, if not his exact words. Though short and succinct in its language, that rule discouraged individualism within the order. It meant to facilitate the flow of alms from West to East, and it was those alms that financed the hospice and the community that staffed it. It also fostered peace among the brothers, and it encouraged poverty and simplicity of life. Above all, it discouraged the accumulation of wealth and power. Frá Gerard's work would only succeed if all worked together, and personal fiefdoms would only inhibit that.

Frá Gerard's teaching became the foundation upon which the order built. Along the way, historical exigencies required course corrections, but each time we have to imagine that the decisions were made with due deliberation. Likely the most far-reaching adjustment was the assumption of military responsibility. Western immigration to the Holy Land was never enough to sustain the Christian "statelets" that emerged. Soon enough, the Knights of St. John were drawn in to supplement the military forces there. That military commitment impacted the order enormously, with repercussions that have reached down even into our own times.

It was not long before the Knights of St. John staffed castles and forts in addition to the hospice. Eventually, however, the Latin colonies in the Holy Land could no longer stem the tide of the Muslim armies. Along with the other Westerners in the Holy Land, the Knights of St. John left first Jerusalem and then the Holy Land altogether. That in turn set in motion a series of difficult decisions about the future of the order.

Could the order survive without a hospice in Jerusalem? Could it carry on from a new base of operations first in Rhodes and then in Malta? Would the military character of the order eclipse the Hospitaller character? Would aristocratic requirements for membership become a permanent feature of the order? Could it survive what seemed to be the loss of everything when Napoleon exiled the order from Malta?

Much as the loss of the Papal States revitalized the public influence of the papacy in the nineteenth century, one can argue that the loss of Malta was not an unmitigated disaster. Through all those centuries, the order had held true to its original mission of service to the sick and the poor. Visitors to Rhodes and Malta can still see the enormous hospitals that the knights left behind, and they testify to the Hospitaller character of the order. If on the one hand there was glamour in the military exploits of the order, one must never forget that knights and grand masters alike took regular turns in serving their lords the sick and the poor in the sacred infirmaries.

From its inception, the Order of St. John did not point its members in the direction of traditional roles of sanctity in the Church, a reason pointed to by Frá Richard in this book for the paucity of knight-saints over a one-thousand-year timeframe. While it did support a few cloisters for women, the order did not expect the knights to live a traditional monastic life. It did not found or conduct schools, nor did it foster intellectual pursuits as the traditional orders did. It did not manage shrines but instead supported pilgrims en route to shrines that others conducted. While it did have priest-chaplains, the order was not a clerical organization headed by a prelate. As a result, the knights did not preach or administer the sacraments.

If traditional paths to sainthood were closed to the Knights of St. John, the order itself was not in a good position to promote members to sainthood. In the twelfth century, popular acclaim served to elevate candidates for sainthood. But the order, with its center in Jerusalem, was hardly able to rely on the local Orthodox Christian and Muslim populations for that acclamation. Residence in Rhodes and Malta did not provide an entirely sympathetic local population either. So the acclamation of saints from within the ranks of the order was left to others rather than directed from the leadership of the order. And finally, one other factor discouraged the proliferation of official sainthood within the order. Many, if not most, people did not think that being a soldier or sailor or diplomat or bureaucrat was the most viable avenue to sainthood.

Given all that, one might marvel that there should be any saints at all in the order. In fact, though, the list of recognized saints could certainly be longer because the roster of those who achieved sanctity through the centuries has to be quite long. That list includes those who sacrificed their lives in witness to their faith. It includes those who quietly worked to facilitate the work of serving the poor and the sick. And most of all, that roster includes all those who saw the vision of the face of Christ in the faces of the sick and the poor. That number continues to grow, and perhaps it now grows exponentially as the order increases in membership.

Frá Gerard is said to have noted that the need for the work of the order will never end. Sadly, the legions of the sick and the poor have scarcely diminished. The good news, however, is that the Lord still calls members to the vineyard. Happily, someday this slim volume on the saints of the order will need a thick supplement that includes the many new saints who will have walked in the steps of Frá Gerard.

Fr. Eric Hollas, OSB

Preface

This work focuses on only a very small number of the thousands of saints that have lived since the beginning of the Christian era: the saints and blessed of the Sovereign Military Order of Malta (SMOM). Included in the following pages are all the saints and blessed who appear in the SMOM Missal, with the addition of Servant of God Frá Andrew Bertie, the seventy-eighth grand master of the order, and Venerable Frá Thomas Dingley, one of the sixteenth-century English martyrs.

The decision to include Frá Andrew is not an attempt to pre-judge the on-going beatification process. Rather, it is a recognition of the influence that he had on the many living members of the order who knew and worked with him. It is a nod to the quiet, yet significant, impact that he had on the order itself, and it's a tribute to his holiness, as perceived by so many of his contemporaries. Writing a book on the order's saints without mention of Frá Andrew just did not seem right.

The idea for this book came at a meeting of the spirituality committee of the American association, one of three associations of the SMOM in the United States. The discussion centered on the lack of any modern, historically accurate work on the saints of the order. The concern was raised that by relying on a few outdated hagiographic treatments of the saints, we might be inadvertently promoting inaccurate and credulous portraits of these holy men and women.

The order's current writings on the saints are, by and large, derived from seventeenth-century hagiographic works which often lack historical sources and tend to accentuate the otherworldliness of the saints. This treatment of the saints as almost ethereal, perfect beings is not only inaccurate but also undermines the notion that all women and men are called to holiness. Our concern was that this antiquated hagiographic treatment, left uncorrected, would continue to leave readers dissatisfied, questioning, and even skeptical. Such an approach to recounting the lives of the saints might not promote disbelief, but it often encourages indifference.

Given this, we agreed that our goal would be to produce a booklet that would employ a modicum of historical scholarship and research, with a particular focus on utilizing scholarly secondary literature. The book also places each saint in his or her historical context to further the reader's understanding of the saint's life. That is not to say that this is an academic monograph. On the contrary, we have cited the secondary literature without actually footnoting references in each chapter to retain simplicity. We wanted to be sure that the book would be accessible and interesting to the reader.

We also wanted the reader to be able to use the book for devotional purposes, so we have included the collect for each saint's feast day. It is my view that historically accurate portrayals of the saints do not undermine piety. Rather, such portrayals promote faith in our intercessors, confidence in our prayers to them, and a realistic acceptance of their human frailties.

We may, in fact, discover in the following pages that there is no historical basis for this story or that miracle. Or there are no existing sources for commonly-held details of a saint's childhood. Or even that there is nothing but oral tradition for us to rely on for information. All this may be the case, but there remains the core message that each individual saint of the order has for us. These messages, which may be different for each saint, do not need to be inflated by fabrications or distorted by exaggeration. The heroic virtues of these saints of the order shine through their life stories, even if those stories, as handed down to us, require some reassessment.

Finally, I must thank several individuals without whom this book could not have been written. Each one assisted me in the early research and provided me with support and encouragement throughout the process: Kenneth Craig, Linda Del Rio, Dr. Thomas Forlenza, Anne Marie Hansen, Mark Kerwin, Peter McGuire, Joseph Metz, Karen Shields, Frá Nicola Tegoni, and Charlotte Williams. Although not historians by training, they each did an excellent job providing me with backup information, outlines, and preliminary research.

I would also like to express my thanks to my editor, Patrick O'Hearn, Frá John Critien, Dr. Peter Kelly, the president of the American Association of the SMOM, for his support and patience, and to Frá Thomas Mulligan, my confrere and president of the Federal Association of the SMOM, for his encouragement. I should also recognize two very important and helpful oral history sources for the chapter on Frá Andrew Bertie: Monsignor Giovanni Scarabelli and Frá James Michael von Stroebel. I am also grateful to Father Eric Hollas, OSB, a fine medieval historian, for his willingness to write the foreword to this book. Notwithstanding the invaluable aid of all these individuals, any errors or omissions are my responsibility.

Frá Richard J. Wolff, PhD

Introduction

"This is the point we very often overlook in the lives of the saints. And it is not always our fault either. The fault is often the biographer's. So many biographers seem so engrossed in impressing their readers with the authentic and genuinely supernatural sanctity of the saints, that the human element is so far omitted or obscured or distorted that mere man is apparently no longer human. While humanity admires, it is at the same time repelled."

—Blessed Miriam Teresa Demjanovich, SC, Convent Station, NJ 1926

This slim volume endeavors to apply current historical scholarship to the study of the saints of the Order of Malta. It is the first comprehensive attempt to do so, although individual saints have been the subject of some excellent scholarly monographs over the last thirty years (e.g., St. Ubaldesca and St. Nuno Alvarez Pereira). The book is organized chronologically not by calendar feast day but into three broad sections: medieval saints (fifth through fourteenth centuries), early modern saints (fifteenth through eighteenth centuries) and modern saints (nineteenth through twenty-first centuries).

The reader will notice that in the modern period, there are several saints who are not normally identified with the Order of Malta; for example, Pope St. Paul VI, Pope St. John XXIII, Blessed Clemens von Galen, and others. Although not a well-known fact, each of the saints included in this grouping was a member of the order, often serving as conventual chaplains or included in the membership because of honors or decorations.

The saints and blessed selected for inclusion in this book are those who have feast days recorded in the Sovereign Military Order of Malta (SMOM) Missal. However, two additional knights, who have not yet been beatified and are not in the SMOM Missal, have been added to the book: Venerable Frá Thomas Dingley and Servant of God Frá Andrew Bertie. Dingley was chosen because of his martyrdom, and Frá Andrew because, as the seventy-eighth grand master of the SMOM, he was known and loved by many people still alive today.

Saints and Martyrs in Late Antiquity

Holy men and women have influenced societies and cultures for thousands of years, not only in the Christian era and not only in the West. Among religions, Catholicism and the Orthodox Church have had the most enduring and sophisticated approach to sanctifying everyday Christians and permitting their veneration. From its very beginning and in an entirely novel way, Christianity emphasized the importance of the saints and their role within the Church. To the faithful, saints were seen as examples of virtue, patrons and intercessors, and sources of miracles. Notably, the concept of the communion of saints was included in the Nicene Creed (AD 325), which articulated the core beliefs of early Christianity. It should not, therefore, be surprising that there remains significant interest in the lives of the holy men and women of the Catholic faith.

The saints of the Order of Malta span the entire length of the order's nine-hundred-year history, from the Middle Ages to the twentieth century. Founded in the twelfth century to care for the poor and sick, the Order of St. John of Jerusalem, as it was then known, quickly added a military arm, extending its charitable activities to include the protection of Christian pilgrims to the Holy Land. The Hospitallers, so called because their first vocation was tending the sick poor in their Jerusalem hospital, began to attract young noblemen and knights, giving rise to a new and unique form of religious life: the military orders, whose role was to take up arms in defense of the Faith against the enemies of Christianity.

Through the years, the cult of saints has played a significant role in the order, but it is curious that the Hospitallers—thousands of whom died over the centuries fighting the Saracens in the Holy Land and on the Mediterranean Sea—never really pursued sainthood for the knights who sacrificed their lives on the battlefield or lost their heads rather than apostatize. This was so even though from the beginning of the Christian era, sainthood was closely linked to martyrdom. Some historians see this reluctance to elevate individual military men to sainthood because of the leadership's concern that in so doing, it would destroy the morale and discipline of the Hospitaller fighting forces (Nicholson 1990). After all, who should be declared a martyr and saint when two hundred fellow knights of the hospital have fallen in battle? Why one knight over another when all could be considered martyrs, a long-standing and traditional path to sainthood in the Church?

In fact, the importance of being designated a "martyr" for the Faith was epitomized by the prominence placed on the early Roman Christian martyrs. By the end of the fourth century, the names of martyred saints began to appear at the celebration of the Eucharist, a practice that remains to this day in the Catholic Mass. Yet, of the order's twenty saints and blessed, only four are classified as martyrs: St. Nicasius of Palermo, Blessed Adrian Fortescue, Blessed David Gonson, and Blessed Vilmos Apor. The fifth martyr is Venerable Thomas Dingley.

The Miraculous Middle Ages

In the early Middle Ages, the popularity of monasticism ushered in a period in which holy men and women were chosen largely from the ranks of ascetic and prayerful hermits and religious, many of whom also displayed extraordinary care and concern for the poor and downtrodden. As the Middle Ages progressed, miracles became an increasingly important part of the requisites for sainthood. A slight majority of the order's saints (ten of eighteen) lived in the medieval period. In many ways, whether according to written sources or oral tradition, they generally conformed to the medieval ideals of sainthood.

St. Ubaldesca, for example, was portrayed as a "saint from the womb," though in truth there is almost nothing known of her childhood. Her asceticism was legendary, and she has been called an example of "holy anorexia" because of her severe, anorexic-like fasting (Bell 1985). All the order's medieval saints were professed religious, apart from St. Ubaldesca and St. Toscana. All, except St. Nicasius, were either women in varying degrees of religious life or male religious whose sanctification came about in large measure due to their service to the sick in the order's hospitals. Not one saint, save for St. Nicasius, was venerated for giving his life in defense of the Faith, although martyrdom was still equated with almost immediate sainthood.

If the people of the Middle Ages expected abundant miracles from their saints, the saints of the order were certainly up to the task. St. Ugo Canefri turned water into wine. St. Toscana brought three men back to life. St. Fleur had the stigmata. St. Ubaldesca was carried to heaven by angels. Blessed Gerland's bones mixed with wine created a blend that cured over one hundred people with various ailments and diseases. The blessed founder, Frá Gerard, turned bread into rocks.

Although the medieval Hospitaller saints, the overwhelming majority of whom were Italian, performed their share of miracles, the appeal of these holy men and women remained largely local and regional. For this reason, they were not of much use to the order for European-wide recruitment, fundraising, or enhancement of the order's reputation—roles that the saints generally played for religious orders at that time. Consequently, for these purposes, the order focused more on promoting its connection to its patron, St. John the Baptist, and its special devotion to the Blessed Virgin Mary, as well as taking some liberties with the facts surrounding its foundation (Nicholson 1990).

The drawbacks of using the Hospitaller saints outside their local areas to further recruitment and fundraising became evident in the twelfth and thirteenth centuries. In stiff competition with other military orders for recruits, alms, and donations, the Hospitallers, like the Templars, began to circulate a history of the order and its origins that was completely fanciful. These contrived stories were designed to attract donations by connecting the order directly to the apostles and to Jesus Christ himself. In these appeals for funding, the first hospital in Jerusalem was said to have been founded at the time of Christ. Christ was supposed to have visited the hospital and to have preached some of his most important sermons there. It was also claimed that Jesus appeared to the apostles at the hospital when, after the Crucifixion, they were cowering behind locked doors.

These stories were apparently (and inexplicably) validated by Pope Clement III at the end of the twelfth century when he said that Christ had indeed visited the Jerusalem hospital while on earth. Master Hugh Revel (1258–1277) promoted these fables, which also included the "fact" that St. John the Baptist's parents visited the hospital and St. Stephen, the first martyr, was familiar with it. This fictional account of the origins of the Knights of St. John apparently circulated among donors and patrons until the late thirteenth century (Nicholson 1990).

Until the mid-fourteenth century, the Church had a method of designating saints that, for the most part, only peripherally involved Rome or the pontiff. It is true that in

1234 Pope Gregory IX issued a set of rules to govern the canonization process, reserving for the pope the right to declare saints. However, this more formal process did not take hold immediately, and the old way remained in place for some time afterward. Under the old way, no real distinction was made between the titles of saint or blessed. Therefore, one should consider these terms interchangeable at least until the mid-fourteenth century, after which the canonization process became somewhat more regulated.

The pre-Gregory IX canonization process was applied to all the order's medieval saints, the last one, St. Fleur, having died around 1347. The process was simple and straightforward. A particular person lived a life of holiness that was recognized by contemporaries. She most likely performed miraculous acts for the benefit of the people, was known for her pious and ascetic life, and had a special love for the poor. Upon her death, the populace would approach the local bishop acclaiming her holiness and asking the bishop to declare her worthy of veneration. If the bishop agreed, the body of the holy woman would be transferred to a shrine, which would become a popular place for prayer, veneration, and often, it was said, multiple miracles (Cunningham 2005).

Only three of the order's saints were women, and all of these women lived in the Middle Ages: St. Ubaldesca, St. Toscana, and St. Fleur. This begs the question, what was the role of women in the medieval Order of St. John? Fortunately, several historians have made the role of Hospitaller women a subject of modern scholarship, shedding light on a neglected area of the order's history (Luttrell and Nicholson 2006).

It appears that women were accepted into the Order of St. John from the very beginning of its foundation. By the thirteenth century, women's status in the order ranged from the fully professed sister to the donat to the consorore or associate. The professed sorores took the evangelical vows of poverty, chastity, and obedience. Of the three female saints of the order, probably only one, St. Fleur, was a vowed religious. St. Toscana was likely a donat, a person who made a commitment to the order, lived in a Hospitaller house, and took the vow of obedience. A consorore lived in her own home, volunteered to work for the order, and was associated with the local Hospitaller preceptory or commandery.

In general, most Hospitaller women did not work in the order's hospitals tending the sick. St. Ubaldesca, for example, may have tended the sick sisters in her convent, but there is no indication in the documents that she spent any time outside working at the order's hospital. The women of the order were more constrained than the men in their living situations. Although not cloistered in the strict sense, the women did not change houses or travel to other convents, nor were they sent from Europe to the Holy Land—all normal activities for the men in the order.

Still, Hospitaller women were not without some standing and privilege within the order. Surprisingly, it was not uncommon for Hospitaller men and women to live in the same house, but in separate quarters. In such a case, the women were apparently permitted to vote for the superior of the house. In Sigena, a Hospitaller convent for women in

Spain, and at convents in Germany, the prioress had authority over the priest-chaplains. There were even instances in which female Hospitallers held commanderies where both men and women lived, giving the prioresses authority over the men of the order. Separate women's houses also existed, and not all of them were cloistered. In fact, in some quarters, the Order of St. John had a reputation for being an easygoing community with many comforts in place for the noble women turned sorores or donats (Luttrell and Nicholson 2006).

On balance, however, the role of female Hospitallers remained traditional. The sorores, who did not do manual labor, were expected to recite the Divine Office each day and to immerse themselves in prayers for the order. Early in its history, the order in Jerusalem had a separate hospital for women, and the patients were cared for by Hospitaller women. Some, but not a majority, of the Hospitaller women continued to work in the order's hospitals or in the commanderies.

For the Hospitallers, their three female saints, Ubaldesca, Toscana, and Fleur, provided examples of holiness to the membership and raised the local profiles of the order among laypersons. The popularity of these saints aided the efforts of Hospitaller women as they sought to persuade their families to fund the construction and upkeep of new houses, to make donations of money and land, or to join the order. In these ways, the Hospitaller women contributed significantly to the financial well-being and growth of the order in the Middle Ages (Nicholson 2010).

Sainthood and the Early Modern Period

The Council of Trent (1545–1563) addressed the issue of canonization in the context of spirited attacks on the concept of sainthood by Protestants, some of whom saw it as nothing short of idolatrous. Sensitive to the credibility issues around some medieval saints, the council reiterated the value of venerating the saints but urged a reform of the canonization process itself. Already in 1588, during the council's deliberations, Pope Sixtus V had issued specific procedures for the canonization process. In 1634, Pope Urban VII made the first formal distinction between blessed and saint, explaining that the former declares a person worthy of local veneration while the latter designates universal veneration.

From 1588 to 1983, the process for canonization was clearly articulated and carefully followed. The Tridentine process began with the local bishop petitioning Rome to begin the investigation of the candidate's life. This petition could only begin fifty years after the candidate's death. When the bishop completed his investigation, and if he decided to go forward, he would send the file to Rome. A postulator would be assigned by the Congregation of Rites (today the Congregation for the Causes of Saints) to defend the cause (the candidacy of the proposed individual). A devil's advocate was appointed to unearth any disqualifying weaknesses in the candidate for sainthood. The completed report then went to the pope, who decided whether the cause should continue. The candidate for sainthood was exhumed, if possible, to check the body for preservation, a sign of holiness. Two miracles were required to attain the title blessed, and two more were necessary to be canonized a saint.

The early modern period also saw the publication of the first known book on the lives of the saints of the order. Giacomo Bosio, a member of the order, wrote *Le Imagini de' Beati Santi della Sacra Religione* in 1622, some sixty years after the close of the council. By this time, the Church had adopted the reformed Tridentine canonization process, which was far more rigorous than the almost informal medieval procedures. Sensitive to the fact that all the order's saints were medieval in origin, Bosio set about to demonstrate that the Hospitaller saints would have been canonized even under the new system (Ebejer 2017). This, however, proved to be a very difficult task.

Biographical details on many of these medieval saints were absent, and sources were not readily found to fill the informational gaps. Bosio did not, however, let this deter him. Like any respectable seventeenth-century hagiographer, he simply manufactured the details to suit his narrative or to fill in the blanks (Cunningham 2005). This work has plagued the order for several hundred years. As a source, Bosio influenced Monsignor Francois Ducaud-Bourget's work, *The Spiritual Heritage of the Sovereign Military Order of Malta* (1958). Ducaud-Bourget accepted much of Bosio's book at face value, thus perpetuating in his own work Bosio's inaccuracies and errors. In turn, Ducaud-Bourget's work today informs much of the order's online and print literature on the holy men and women of the order.

At the same time, the early modern period also saw the first advances of historical scholarship around the saints. The Jesuit Jean Bolland (1596–1665) inherited the project from his brother Jesuit Heribert Rosweyde, who had begun to gather documentation to support biographies of the saints but died prematurely in 1629. Bolland recruited several other Jesuit scholars who searched libraries and archives throughout Europe to better document the lives of the saints. These followers were referred to as the Bollandists. They utilized this documentation to supplant, when appropriate, unreliable information about the saints in many hagiographies. The product of this effort was a two-volume work, *Acta Sanctorum*, published in 1643. By 1681, twenty-two subsequent volumes had been added to the original two. Further volumes were published in the nineteenth century, and the work of the Bollandists on critical hagiography continues to this day.

The *Acta* conflicts with the order's traditional hagiographies in at least three instances. It states that Blessed Gerard Mecatti was not a knight of St. John but rather a member of the Franciscan Third Order. It suggests that Blessed Gerland was likely a Templar, not a Hospitaller, and it makes no mention at all of St. Nicasius. Historians take a variety of positions on the accuracy of the *Acta* in these instances, but these assertions do question the traditional Hospitaller narrative and must be acknowledged.

The order had three recognized martyrs for the Faith in the sixteenth century: Blessed Adrian Fortesque, Blessed David Gonson, and Venerable Thomas Dingley. All three were victims of the wrath of Henry VIII, and all three refused offers of freedom in return for renouncing the pope and Rome. Normally, a book on the saints of the order would not include those with the title of venerable, but Frá Dingley's status as a martyr merits his inclusion.

As martyrs who died rather than deny the Faith, these three knights followed a long Hospitaller tradition. Unlike their predecessors in the order, however, their sacrifices were recognized and venerated. At the time of the English martyrs, it had been almost four hundred years since the last Hospitaller martyr, St. Nicasius, had lived. As the early modern period drew to a close, the order increased the ranks of its holy men with these three courageous English knights. It would be another four hundred years before the order had its fifth martyr, Bishop Vilmos Apor.

Apart from martyrs, saints in the early modern period generally came from the ranks of men and women religious reformers, champions of the Catholic Counter-Reformation, and evangelizers to the New World or to Protestant enclaves in Europe. It must be said that the Order of Malta contributed many unrecognized martyrs in its storied defense of Malta and Christendom from the Saracen onslaught in 1565.

Still, the Hospitallers did not necessarily display the characteristics that early modern Europe preferred in its saints. Saints were being made who waged sophisticated intellectual war against the reformers (St. Robert Bellarmine), or founded militant religious orders intent on turning the Protestant tide (St. Ignatius Loyola), or reclaimed lost souls and territory for the Catholic faith (St. Peter Claver), or led the religious renewal that swept Europe in the years following Trent (St. Francis de Sales).

As time passed, the Muslim threat to Christian Europe diminished, eventually depriving the order of its military raison d'être. It continued its commitment to the poor and sick, but the heroic deeds suitable for the new era were not the focus of the order. It was neither trained for "peaceful evangelization" of the Protestants nor was it interested in the religious wars spawned by the Reformation, since it was expressly forbidden by its own rule to take up arms against other Christians. In short, without recourse to its military, the Hospitallers, lacking a tradition of theological or philosophical disputation, were in no position to contribute much to the battle against the Protestant heresies threatening the unity of Latin Christendom.

From the sixteenth through the nineteenth centuries, the order did not produce another recognized saint. It was not until the twentieth century, which saw a growing openness in the Church to the canonization of lay persons and a renewed emphasis on social justice, that saints and blesseds once again arose in the order.

The Modern Period

Of the six saints and blesseds in the modern period, all lived their adult lives in the twentieth century, and all were directly impacted by World War I or World War II. Given their prominent positions in society and the Church, they were active with the order in varying degrees. Only one was a layperson, Blessed Charles, the last ruler of the Austro-Hungarian Empire. Except for the emperor, who died in 1922, all the saints and blessed were in positions of responsibility during the rise of European fascist and Nazi regimes, World War II, and the Holocaust.

The two pope-saints, John XXIII and Paul VI, together were the architects of Vatican II and the subsequent renewal of the universal Church. They regularly reminded the faithful, many of whom were shaken by the reforms of Vatican II, of the importance of the intercession of the Blessed Virgin Mary and the saints. It was well-known that Pope John held a special place in his heart for St. Francis of Assisi, and Pope Paul, despite the opposition of some churchmen, dedicated the universal Church to Mary in 1964. Both popes, but especially Paul, were intensely focused on social justice, the north-south divide in global wealth, and the preferential option for the poor.

In *Lumen Gentium*, the Second Vatican Council issued a universal call to holiness, a call to all men and women to live "as becomes saints . . . to have a beloved heart of mercy, kindness, humility, meekness, and patience." Everyone, said the council fathers, is called to sainthood, to "follow in Christ's footsteps and devote ourselves to the Glory of God and service to our neighbors." Vatican II made it clear that sainthood was not confined to a small number of clerics or religious, even if over the centuries saints who were priests, nuns, and brothers dwarfed the number of laypersons. The council called everyone in the Church to holiness and, therefore, to sainthood. Holiness was not to be thought of as being beyond the layperson's capability. Blessed Charles of Austria, who could not have been more involved in the most important events of his time, was a good example of this call to holiness, even though he died forty years before the council issued it.

The modern period also saw the reform of the Tridentine canonization process, with the goal to make it less onerous. In 1983, Pope John Paul II promulgated new procedures in his encyclical *Divinus Perfectionis Magister*. The pope shifted the investigative responsibility back to local bishops instead of centering it in Rome. In a sense, this was a return to the medieval practice in that it enhanced the role of the local ordinaries. The bishops then send their completed investigations to the Congregation for the Causes of Saints in Rome. The congregation appoints a relator who is responsible for drawing up a biography, with supporting documentation, of the candidates for sainthood. Once theologians approve the candidates, their miracles are examined by a panel of independent doctors and scientists. Instead of a total of four miracles under the Tridentine process, two are required: one for beatification and a second for canonization.

The beatifications of the prelates Schuster, von Galen, and Apor allowed the Church to make a serious point concerning one of the late twentieth century's most controversial questions: Had the Church done enough to stand for morality and human rights in the face of Nazi terror and the Holocaust (Wolff and Hoensch 1987)? The lives of these three generally conservative bishops illustrate the significant Church opposition to the Nazis and their racial theories. In the case of von Galen, his outspoken defiance and condemnation of racial theories and euthanasia occurred right under Hitler's nose, and it did not go unnoticed. Hitler made it clear that he would settle scores with the Church and von Galen after the war. Fortunately, there was no after the war for Hitler. In the period between the two world wars, the Hungarian bishop Vilmos Apor worked tirelessly among the poor herded into cheap government housing on the outskirts of the cities. He was outspoken on the issues of the day and vigorously opposed both Nazi and Communist influence in Hungary. He became the order's fifth martyr when he was killed by invading Soviet troops in 1945.

Significantly, miracles do not play an outsized role in the beatification process in the modern period. As long as the requirement of one attributed miracle could be met, the process would stay on track. Far more important was having lived a life of heroic virtue to which the faithful could relate and ultimately imitate. As the call to holiness resonated more loudly within the Church, the traditional saint's role as a model for the virtuous life took on more importance than ever.

In the twentieth century, the order's saints and blesseds were men who, when confronted with the pervasive evils of Nazism and Communism, spoke out for justice. While others feared for their lives, families, and property, these men raised their voices against racism, atheism, and totalitarianism. They provide examples of love, courage, patience, humility, perseverance, and faithfulness whether wrestling with social evils and injustices, practicing the preferential option for the poor, or guiding the Church through its most important renewal in centuries.

From the twelfth century to the twentieth century, this display of heroic virtue has been what binds together the order's holy men and women. Medieval or modern, a life of heroic virtue and a love for the poor and sick were common characteristics of the saints of the order. In the end, there is no need to exaggerate their lives, amplify their miracles, or take liberties with the facts. These twenty men and women lived exemplary lives of holiness, lives that are worthy of imitation, despite all their imperfections and human limitations.

Medieval Saints

The Fifth through the Fourteenth Centuries

Blessed Gerard, Founder

Died Circa 1120

B lessed Gerard founded the Hospitaller Order of St. John (later known as the Order of Malta) in the mid-eleventh century, circa 1070. He died in Jerusalem around 1120.

Nothing is known of the early life of Blessed Gerard; his date of birth and surname remain a mystery. However, historians have pieced together reliable, if limited, information about his adult life in Jerusalem from around 1060 to his death. Gerard lived in a violent and war-torn century marked by the bloody First Crusade (1096–1099), which returned Jerusalem to Christendom after over four hundred years of Muslim control.

From the fourth century onwards, a pilgrimage to Jerusalem was regarded as the most effective way of ensuring the forgiveness of sins, and thousands of Christians made the perilous journey annually. An extraordinary number of pilgrims began streaming into Jerusalem around the year 1000, very likely reflecting the popular expectation that the new millennium would usher in the second coming of Christ.

The relatively high numbers of pilgrims to the Holy Land persisted, only slightly diminished, throughout the eleventh century.

As the eleventh century progressed, travel to the Holy Land became increasingly dangerous for pilgrims. The safety of the millennial pilgrims was insured by the 1001 treaty between Byzantine emperor Basil II and the caliph al-Hakim bi-Amr Allah (985–1021), but this fragile agreement was broken by al-Hakim in 1009 when he turned on the Christians and destroyed the Church of the Holy Sepulchre. In 1065, a large contingent of German pilgrims was set upon by Muslim outlaws, and two-thirds of the Christians were killed. In the wake of the disastrous Christian defeat at Manzikert in 1071, the Byzantine emperors gradually lost control of Anatolia to the Seljuk Turks, making the pilgrim route to Jerusalem more perilous than ever.

The danger of traveling to the Holy Land did not, however, deter the Italian trading cities from opening and plying trade routes between the Levant and Europe. Writing in the twelfth century, William, archbishop of Tyre, asserts that around the mid-eleventh century, a group of traders from Amalfi petitioned the caliph of Egypt, who at the time had suzerainty over Jerusalem, for a place where their fellow countrymen could stay when in the holy city. According to William, the caliph gave them a site near the Church of the Holy Sepulchre. The Amalfitans built a church (The Church of the Redeemer), a monastery (St. Mary of the Latins), and a convent (dedicated to St. Mary Magdelene). The brothers in St. Mary of the Latins, likely including Frá Gerard, subsequently constructed a hospital and dedicated it to St.

John the Baptist. These dedications were probably no coincidence, since the cathedral in Amalfi was named in honor of both the Blessed Virgin and St. John the Baptist.

Historians generally agree that the Hospital of St. John was established just prior to 1070. This approximate date is based on the anonymous Amalfitan chronicler who wrote that the archbishop of Amalfi, John, made a pilgrimage to Jerusalem in the 1070s. He was hosted by the Amalfitan community and saw the Hospital of St. John and a second hospital for women. This chronicle also attests to the fact that the hospitals were staffed by at least quasi-religious who took some form of the evangelical vows and wore religious garb. Given that the archbishop toured the hospitals in the 1070s, it is plausible to date the establishment of the Hospital of St. John to this approximate period.

Since the hospitals were founded by the serving brothers of the Benedictine Monastery of St. Mary of the Latins, it is likely that the nascent, quasi-religious community, which was growing around the hospital serving the poor and sick, was initially influenced by the Benedictine rule. The first superior of the hospital community was Frá Gerard, whom chroniclers identify as being in office before and after the First Crusade. Pope Paschal II, in his bull *Pie postulation voluntatis* (1113), recognized Frá Gerard as the founder and superior of the Hospital of St. John. Most medieval scholars agree that Gerard was an Amalfitan serving brother, perhaps even an ex-merchant, living at St. Mary of the Latins.

Frá Gerard established the Hospital of St. John as a religious association at a time when Benedictine influence on Latin religious life, which had held sway since the early ninth century, was waning. By the mid-eleventh century, the seeds of the foundation of new religious communities were sown, and alongside the Hospitallers would come the Templars, Dominicans, Franciscans, Cistercians, and Carthusians. Frá Gerard was an early founder of a new type of religious order that focused on not only internal monastic life but also active pastoral ministries—in this case, serving the poor and sick.

By the eve of the First Crusade, with Jerusalem still in the hands of the Muslims, Frá Gerard had established a large, well-functioning hospital serving pilgrims to the Holy Land and the sick and poor of any religion. In addition to ministering to the sick, the hospital was charged with burying the indigent dead. Frá Gerard taught his followers to see Christ in every poor patient brought to the hospital, regardless of race or religion. Recognizing Christ in the sick poor meant that Frá Gerard's followers regarded them as their "lords" and provided superior standards of care, as if they were ministering to Christ himself. Jonathan Riley Smith, a medievalist, described the unique features of the Jerusalem hospital:

> The great hospital in Jerusalem . . . could accommodate 2,000 patients, male and female. . . . There were separate beds for the sick at a time when only the grandest lords had their own beds (and in the obstetrical ward there were little cots so that the babies should not be disturbed by their mothers). The beds had feather mattresses and coverlets, and the patients were provided with cloaks and sandals, so as to protect

them when they went to the latrines. . . . The diet provided was lavish. . . . At a time when very few people
had white bread . . . or a meat diet, white bread was
served . . . together with fresh meat on three days a
week. (Riley-Smith 1994)

The hospital's medical care, although primitive, was state-
of-the-art for its time. Physicians were assigned to specific
wards to ensure consistency in patient care, and they were
required to make rounds twice daily. The hospital also had
a robust outreach program throughout the city. Frá Gerard
sent the brothers into the neighborhoods of the city looking
for the poor too ill to make it on their own to the hospital.
They also delivered clothes and alms to the poor, especially
to pregnant women, regardless of religion.

When the Christian siege of Jerusalem began in 1099,
Gerard was presumably a well-known figure in the city.
During the siege, he was said to have been imprisoned and
tortured, but historians can find no record of this, except
oral tradition. Anticipating the siege, the Muslims destroyed
foodstuff, killed livestock, and poisoned drinking wells outside the walls to deprive the crusaders of sustenance. Frá
Gerard is said to have gathered loaves of bread in his cloak
and, under the cover of darkness, tossed them over the wall
to the hungry Christian besiegers. Caught in the act by a
Muslim guard, he was ordered to open his cloak to reveal
what he had been throwing over the wall. When he did,
stones, instead of bread, miraculously fell to the ground, and
the Muslims were forced to release him.

The chronicles are silent on the activities of Frá Gerard and the hospital at the fall of Jerusalem and the subsequent horrific slaughter of the Muslim population, but it is safe to assume that the brothers' hospital played a major role in caring for the wounded on both sides. The return of Christian political power to the Levant meant that the responsibility for the Church of the Holy Sepulchre was transferred from the Syrian Christians to the Latin Church. Frá Gerard and his brothers came under the authority of the Latin patriarch (the papal representative in the Holy Land) and his canons (priests living in community according to a particular rule) now seated at the Church of the Holy Sepulchre. This is evident because many donations, which began to pour into the Hospital of St. John after the victorious crusade, were legally given over to "the Hospital of St. John of Jerusalem and the Church of the Holy Sepulchre," as if these two institutions were one and the same.

Further, Frá Gerard's nascent community began to receive property bequests in Europe, led by Godfrey of Bouillon's gift of the manor of Montboise in Brabant, a province in the Low Countries. The high regard with which the new Christian ruler of the Levant held the hospital did not go unnoticed by other great lords. Gifted land and properties rapidly enriched the young fraternity under Frá Gerard, and its ranks were swelled by crusaders who now laid down their arms to take up the life of Hospitallers. Frá Gerard offered a new type of religious vocation that attracted the crusaders: one that allowed a religious life while preserving an active role in the world.

Oddly enough, the Hospitallers of the latter twelfth century (Geroh, provost of Reichersberg, for example) promoted various fantastical stories about the origin of the Hospital of St. John of Jerusalem. Apparently, to compete in fundraising with other religious orders, some members asserted that the hospital existed in the time of the Apostles. Others claimed that the parents of St. John the Baptist served the poor at the hospital. Still others insisted that Christ himself visited the hospital and performed many miracles there. Suffice to say that these outlandish claims asserting the pre-patristic roots of the hospital did not stand the test of time, and the documents clearly point to Frá Gerard as the founder of the hospital in Jerusalem and the Order of St. John.

It was also at this time that the canons of the Church of the Holy Sepulchre seem to have exerted some influence on the rule by which Frá Gerard's community lived. Perhaps the canons, who followed the Rule of St. Augustine, brought this religious lifestyle to their relationship with the hospital, thus edging out the Benedictine traditions. This is evident from the fact that the first written Hospitaller rule of Master Raymond du Puy, given in the twelfth century, was significantly influenced by the Rule of St. Augustine. In this, the hospital was following a European trend away from the Rule of St. Benedict and towards the Rule of St. Augustine, the latter being seen as more modern and suitable to an increasingly urban and literate society.

With the new Christian state established and his fraternity of brothers flourishing, Frá Gerard sought papal approval for his hospital and recognition as a religious order. The hospital had, in effect, been operating as a quasi-religious order for

several decades under Frá Gerard, with members living the
three evangelical vows of poverty, chastity, and obedience
and wearing black habits with the eight-pointed white cross.
It had also been slowly gaining financial independence from
the Latin hierarchy. But Frá Gerard was seeking the security
of papal recognition and papal privileges for his community,
both of which were conferred by Pope Paschal II in 1113.

Paschal's bull *Pie postulation voluntatis* recognized the
Hospital of St. John of Jerusalem as a religious order. It
exempted the order from the payment of the tithe, recognized its independence from the Monastery of St. Mary
Latin, confirmed the significant gifts it had received, and
established its independence from local bishops. The Hospitallers, as they would become known, were granted the
privilege of electing their own Master without episcopal
interference. The bull also acknowledged a new direction
for religious orders: international in scope but centralized
in governance. All rights and privileges granted by the bull
applied to the entire order, including its preceptories (pilgrim houses set up at points of embarkation for the Holy
Land) outside the Levant. The twelfth century saw succes-
sive popes confirm and expand the privileges of the order,
essentially exempting them from all ecclesiastic interference,
save that of the pope himself.

Frá Gerard did not live to see the development of the
order's formidable military capabilities and the rise of its role
and reputation as the great defender of Christendom. He died
sometime between 1118 and 1120. After his death, Blessed
Gerard was likely proclaimed a saint by acclamation of the
Christian community, which was often the case in the early

medieval period. By 1283, his preserved body had been transferred from the Levant to Provence due to the deteriorating position of the Kingdom of Jerusalem. His remains were desecrated and destroyed during the French Revolution, but his skull was saved and is in the Monastery of St. Ursula in Malta.

Although well-known for his outstanding organizational skills that laid the foundation for over nine hundred years of Hospitallers, Blessed Gerard was above all admired by his contemporaries for his humility and his intense love of the poor. William of Tyre called him a venerable and pious man, and his epitaph read, "Here lies Gerard, the humblest man in the East, the servant of the poor, hospitable to strangers, meek of countenance but with a noble heart. One can see in these walls how good he was. He was provident and active. Exerting himself in all sorts of ways, he stretched forth his arms into many lands to obtain what he needed to feed his own. On the seventeenth day of the passage of the sun under the sign of Virgo (September 3), he was carried into heaven by the hands of the angels."

The blessed founder's feast day is celebrated on October 13.

Collect From the Missal of the Sovereign Military Order of Malta

O God, who raised up Blessed Gerard because of his wondrous care for the poor and sick, and through him founded the Order of St. John in Jerusalem, grant we pray that, following his example, we may always see the image of your Son in our brothers and sisters. Through Our Lord, Jesus Christ, your Son, who lives and reigns with you in the unity of the Holy Spirit, One God forever and ever.

2

St. Ubaldesca of Calcinaia

Circa 1145–1205/6

St. Ubaldesca was born around 1145 in the rural village of Calcinaia, which is east of Pisa in the region of Tuscany. She entered the Monastery of St. John around 1159 and spent the rest of her life in Pisa. She died in 1205.

In the case of many medieval saints, primary source documentation is not only scarce but also difficult to accurately interpret. St. Ubaldesca is no exception to this rule. On the life of Ubaldesca, there is one principal source written in 1593 by Silvio Razzi that has, with uneven outcomes, influenced much of the hagiographic literature surrounding Ubaldesca. There is also another manuscript that includes a copy of an original Vita, or biography, of Ubaldesca translated from Latin to Italian. This manuscript dates from the mid-sixteenth century. Modern historians have used these and other documents, such as Archbishop Frederico Visconti's 1263 sermon, to arrive at a more accurate understanding of the life and significance of St. Ubaldesca.

In the mid-twelfth century, Castello di Calcinaia was an administrative part of the prosperous Republic of Pisa (ca. 1000–1406). Ubaldesca's birthplace was a poor rural district of the Republic, and many peasants were migrating during this period from farms to the burgeoning city in search of better lives. Little is known of the early life of Ubaldesca. Her parents are unnamed, although there are some medievalists who believe her family name was Taccini (Zaccagnini 1995).

Much of the hagiographic treatment of Ubaldesca's child-hood was written with the intention of establishing her as a "saint from her mother's womb," but it is unsupported by any documentation. Because contemporary medieval soci-ety viewed the rural poor as untrustworthy, duplicitous, and ignorant, early hagiographers, in an effort to counter this view, portrayed Ubaldesca's parents as examples of simple and virtuous Christian probity (Zaccagnini 1995). This is not to say that Ubaldesca's home life was not exemplary and supportive of her vocation. It is merely a recognition that there is a dearth of evidence and reliable sources for this period of Ubaldesca's life.

At the age of fourteen, Ubaldesca entered the Monastery of St. John in Pisa. This was a somewhat unlikely choice for the young girl from the peasant class, without education or dowry, as many of the nuns would have been of aristocratic or at least bourgeois origin. The earliest accounts of this decision to enter the monastery speak of Ubaldesca's vision of an angel who urged her to go immediately to Pisa where the nuns would be waiting for her.

Protesting her unsuitability (the lack of proper family ori-gins and a dowry), Ubaldesca told the angel that entering the Monastery of St. John was not possible, but the angel insisted that the sisters needed her simplicity and virtue and were awaiting her arrival. She left hurriedly to find her parents, and they together rushed to the monastery. Ubaldesca had left, however, bread baking in the oven. When her parents returned to their hut the next day, they found the bread had not burned but was baked to perfection. They took the bread to the monastery as sign of the favor God had bestowed on Ubaldesca.

The vision of the angel and the miracle of the bread were powerful signs to medieval society that vocations did not always have to originate among the nobility or commercial aristocracy. Years later, while in the monastery, Ubaldesca was credited with a Christ-like miracle on a Good Friday— turning water into wine—and she suffered an open wound on her head, as a penance she said, for many years after being struck by a falling stone from a building façade. These, and many other miracles, bolstered the view that poor young women, virtuous in their simplicity and modesty, could be called by God not only to enter convents but also, like Ubaldesca, to become great and influential saints.

When Ubaldesca entered the monastery in Pisa, it was most likely not yet affiliated with the Order of St. John of Jerusalem. There are no documents pertaining to the monastery prior to 1207, but there are references beginning in that year to the male community of Hospitallers at St. Sepolcro and the female Hospitallers at the Monastery of St. John, both in Pisa. Medievalists believe that Ubaldesca's monastery was probably not a Hospitaller community when Ubaldesca entered because it was in such dire financial straits, a condition that the wealthy Order of St. John would never have permitted (Zaccagnini 1995).

The poverty of the sisters forced Ubaldesca into the streets to beg for alms to help sustain the community. Further, the monastery seems to have had the typical mission of religious houses of this period: to welcome all travelers and those who were poor, indigent, weak, widowed, or orphaned who came to its doors. It did not have a hospital attached to it, like Order of St. John houses, until years after Ubaldesca's death. It is likely, then, that Ubaldesca entered a feminine community of unknown origin that, by 1207, two years after her death, had fully integrated into the Order of St. John.

There is also some question as to whether, as later hagiographers claimed, Ubaldesca was a religious who took the evangelical vows. There are several reasons why some medievalists contend that she may well have been a "lay penitent" or oblate rather than a religious sister. It is important to note that although formal training or novitiates in the mid-twelfth century were not usual, there was a modicum of education expected of those women who took vows as religious. Ubaldesca was a peasant girl educated, if at all, by her likely illiterate parents when she presented herself to the abbess in 1159. It is probable that she was taken in as a lay penitent, permitted to live out her life with the sisters, following the rule of the house. This would explain how she was admitted without a dowry to a poor convent desperately in need of financial assistance and why, unlike any of the sisters, she was permitted to leave the monastery regularly to beg for alms in the streets of Pisa (Zaccagnini 1995).

Whether or not Ubaldesca was a bona fide religious, she apparently lived a life of heroic virtue that was widely recognized by her contemporaries. Although there is no evidence that she served the sick and poor directly, except for caring for the ill sisters in the monastery's infirmary, Ubaldesca was a familiar figure in the streets of Pisa, asking for alms and displaying a humble and devout demeanor.

Piety was often expressed during the twelfth and thirteenth centuries as "imitating" Christ, and this included his suffering. Ubaldesca fasted and practiced severe acts of mortification in pursuit of the imitation of Christ. Her fasting was so severe that modern scholars have listed her as the first "holy anorexic," women who exhibited symptoms of anorexia in their pursuit of holiness. When Ubaldesca died rather suddenly in 1205 or 1206, there were reports of many miracles at her tomb. The abbess and sisters of her convent claim to have witnessed her body being carried to the heavens by a host of angels.

The monastery at around the time of Ubaldesca's death was just beginning to come under the aegis of the Order of Malta. However, the order began laying claim to Ubaldesca's fame as a holy woman even before she died and well before the miracles involving any Hospitallers.

Frá Dotto degli Occhi, a professed chaplain of the order resident at the Monastery and Church of St. Sepolcro, was the most ardent supporter of Ubaldesca's growing reputation for saintliness among the local populace. At her death, this well-known adherent of Ubaldesca spent seven days in constant vigil at her original tomb, where she was placed by the sisters of the Monastery of St. John. On the seventh day, Ubaldesca was said to be seen by many witnesses being raised again from the tomb in the company of angels. Frá Dotto immediately claimed this second rising signified that Ubaldesca's body should be exhumed and brought to the Hospitaller monastery and church.

Although Ubaldesca no longer rested with her sisters, the Monastery of St. John very soon after her death became a part of the Order of St. John. In 1564, the saint's head was apparently returned to the Monastery of St. John. In the ensuing decades, this holy peasant woman, whose intercession apparently resulted in numerous cures and other miracles after her death, became known as a saint of the Order of St. John.

One of her later miracles apparently involved the prior of St. Sepolcro, the Hospitaller convent and church with an attached hospital. For some reason, the prior was unceremoniously dismissed in 1396 by the grand master. This was likely because the Western Church had competing popes: Clement VII and Urban VI. This gave rise to rival grand masters in the order, with Juan Hernandez de Heredia and Riccardo Carraciolo claiming the position. The prior, Frá Bartolo, may have found himself on the wrong side of this schism. Embarrassed and humiliated by his sudden ouster, he prayed to Ubaldesca to help him to be restored to his position.

Ubaldesca is said to have appeared to Frá Bartolo in a vision, and he promised her that if he were restored at the priory, he would celebrate a solemnity to her every Holy Trinity Sunday. In fact, Frá Bartolo was reappointed as prior, and the feast of St. Ubaldesca is celebrated on Holy Trinity

Sunday to this day. These miracles involving Hospitallers helped to cement the tenuous links between the order and Ubaldesca.

In 1587, in an effort to further solidify its claim on medieval Hospitaller saints, the order petitioned Rome, requesting that some of Ubaldesca's remains be transferred from Pisa to the island of Malta. Pope Sixtus V granted the order's request while at the same time affirming Ubaldesca's status as a saint in a breve considered equivalent to a canonization. The saint's arm, however, was left in the cathedral in Pisa, and her head in the Monastery of St. John. In 1810, the spread of political influence of the French Revolution resulted in the suppression of the Monastery at St. John, and Ubaldesca's remains were sent to St. Sepolcro. In 1924, after hundreds of years of requests and with great fanfare, St. Ubaldesca's remains were gathered and sent to rest in St. John the Baptist Church in the town of her birth, Calcinaia.

St. Ubaldesca, most likely a lay woman living as an oblate or even servant among professed nuns, achieved a status among her contemporaries that recognized her holiness long before the institutional Church. Her apparent humility and simplicity attracted many followers who attested to the miracles attributed to her intercession. Ubaldesca's low social status as an illiterate, uneducated peasant girl did not, surprisingly, result in rejection from the convent or resentment among the sophisticated urban class of Pisa. Rather, she was, for many of her contemporaries, an example of how even the most disadvantaged lay people—not only clerics, nobles and the commercial classes—could imitate the life of Christ and aspire to spiritual greatness and personal holiness.

St. Ubaldesca died in 1205. Her feast day is May 28.

Collect From the Missal of the Sovereign
Military Order of Malta

O God, exaltation of the lowly and lover of virginity, who were pleased to call the Virgin Saint Ubaldesca to religious life in the Order of Saint John of Jerusalem, mercifully grant that, through her intercession and example, we may rejoice in humility and follow you with pure hearts. Through our Lord Jesus Christ, your Son, who lives and reigns with you in the unity of the Holy Spirit, one God, forever and ever.

3

St. Ugo Canefri

Circa 1168–1233

St. Ugo Canefri, also known as St. Hugo of Genoa, was born around 1168 in the town of Alessandria, Italy. He entered the Order of Saint John at about the age of nineteen and eventually pledged the evangelical vows as a professed Knight of Justice. He fought in the Third Crusade (1189–1192) and returned to Italy to serve the poor and sick. He died in Genoa in 1233.

Although Ugo lived in the late twelfth and early thirteenth centuries, there are several chronicles and brief early biographies of the saint. The chronicle of G. Antonio Clari, written in 1233 shortly after Frá Ugo's death, has provided much detail to subsequent historians and biographers. The Dominican Frá Lorenzo Feo cited Clari in his book *Italia Famose*, written in 1483. Giacomo Bosio featured Frá Ugo prominently in his 1594 work *Storia dell Sacra Religione ed Illustri milizia de San Giovanni Gerosolimitano*, again drawing upon the early chronicles.

In 1665, the Italian poet Giambattista Vedura penned a poem entitled *Vita, Morte e Miracoli di Sant'Ugo, Cavalliere*. The popularity of this work, four hundred years after the death of Frá Ugo, attests to the saint's enduring place in Italian piety, especially in northern Italy. In 1887, a fairly complete biography of Ugo appeared in Vincenzo Persoglio's *Sant'Ugo e la Commenda de San Giovanni di Prè*. In short, recounting the life of Saint Ugo, who lived 820 years ago, although not without difficulty, is less fraught with factual dilemmas and inconclusive historical arguments than some of the order's other medieval saints. One issue, however, was not put to rest until Persoglio's work in the late nineteenth century. A minority of hagiographers insisted that Ugo was born in France, a position that did not hold up under Persoglio's analysis.

With the birthplace issue defused, the major arc of Ugo's life is well settled. He was born of a noble family, the Canefris, around 1168 in the newly established town of Alessandria. Some historians think that chroniclers settled on the year 1168 because that year marked the founding of the new fortified town. In any case, it is agreed that if his birth was not in 1168, it was very close to that year. Alessandria, likely named for Pope Alexander III whose papacy lasted from 1159 to his death in 1181, was established as a free commune with Genoa as its overlord. This meant that political power, although formally vested in the bishop, was held by the leading townsmen who voted for their podesta, or mayor. The Canefris, in the person of Ugo's father, Count Arnoldo Canefri Gamondio, took a major role in the establishment of the town.

Northern Italy in the twelfth century was wracked by the conflict between the popes, whose supporters were known as Guelfs, and the German Holy Roman emperors, whose adherents were termed Ghibellines. Alessandria was built by the Guelf faction, part of the Lombard League, to control the access ways to Genoa and Torino. The well-fortified town was equidistant, about fifty-five miles, from Genoa and Torino. Emperor Frederick Barbarossa's imperial troops laid siege to the town in 1174. Ugo Canefri was about six years old when the town came under attack. Alessandria remained firm, as malaria spread through the emperor's army. His forces weakened by disease and mistakenly thinking that the town was better supplied than it was, Frederick raised the unsuccessful siege in 1175.

The earliest chronicles tell little of Ugo's boyhood, but there is no doubt that his family was among the most prominent in the region. The Canefri family seems to have held very important positions in both the Church and state. During Ugo's lifetime, family members were apparently consuls, or mayors, in Alessandria three times for a total of forty-six years. The *Annali di Alessandria*, published in 1666, lists at least one Canefri cardinal, Pietro, from 1183–1192. According to other sources, there may well have been two other cardinals in the extended family. In 1243, some twenty years after Ugo's death, Sinbaldo Fieschi, a maternal relative of Ugo's, was elected to the papal throne, taking the name Innocent IV.

Ugo's education likely followed that of most male children of noble families. He was probably taught hunting, horsemanship, the art of warfare, basic reading and writing in

Latin and the vernacular, and rudimentary arithmetic. Even though this was the general norm for the time, it was not always followed by the nobility. In fact, it was not unheard of that some Hospitaller knights were barely literate. However, given the role and status of the Canefri family as consuls and cardinals, it is unlikely that Ugo's education was neglected. When at around the age of nineteen he asked to be admitted to the Order of St. John, Ugo was most likely a reasonably educated, idealistic young man, well-skilled in the martial arts and eager to serve God as a crusader.

There is not a great deal of detail known about Ugo's experience in the Third Crusade (1189–1192). The Crusade was preached by Pope Gregory VIII in 1187. Gregory called for a holy war to take back Jerusalem, which had fallen to the legendary Saladin, sultan of Egypt and Syria, earlier that year. Ugo answered the papal summons along with hundreds of others from Genoa and its surrounding towns and villages. Ugo is said to have entered the Order of St. John sometime during his stay in the Holy Land.

The Third Crusade pitted a formidable coalition of Christians, led by Emperor Frederick I (Barbarossa), King Philip II of France, and King Richard I of England against Saladin. The Crusade was marred by misfortune from its very beginning when, in 1190, the emperor drowned in transit to the Holy Land. Nevertheless, under the capable generalship of Richard, the crusaders met with initial success, taking the important city of Acre in July 1191. A month later, King Philip was compelled to return to France to manage a political crisis threatening his rule. Nonetheless, Richard pressed on, retaking Jaffa from Saladin in July 1192.

The crusaders were meeting with success on the battlefield, but their ranks were being decimated by disease. With his armies encamped in sight of Jerusalem, Richard was forced to confront the fact that even if he took the city, the Christians would not be able to hold it. He consulted with the masters of the Hospitallers and Templars, who both agreed with his assessment. Richard then negotiated a treaty with Saladin, leaving a small area of the former Kingdom of Jerusalem and the city of Acre in Christian hands. The agreement, which was merely a truce, also ensured protection for Christian pilgrims.

Now a knight of St. John, Ugo returned to Genoa, probably sometime after 1195. He had taken part in an only marginally successful Crusade, but one in which European contemporaries celebrated the valor and bravery of the Hospitallers. For the first time, the Hospitallers were viewed as matching the Templars in military prowess. During the Crusade, the Order of St. John participated in the highest councils of war, its army played a central role in many battles and sieges, its navy was pivotal in the battle for Tyre, and its fortresses, like Margat, were considered unassailable—even by Saladin himself. It is not possible to know how Ugo was impacted by this wartime experience, but once back in Alessandria and Genoa, Frá Ugo never again participated in a military campaign.

Historians (Persoglio 1878) tend to believe that sometime between 1198 and 1201, the order put Frá Ugo in charge of the commandery of San Giovanni di Prè in Genoa, which included a church and a hospital. The order's commanderies were expected to produce income for their commanders, usually professed knights, and to generate dues for the central convent. Although he was admittedly young for such a prize, it was probably not unexpected given the status of his family in Alessandria and Genoa, as well as its influence in Rome.

The twelfth and early thirteenth centuries were in some ways a difficult time to be a member of the military orders. Throughout much of the twelfth century, outspoken clergymen and others questioned the legitimacy of religious orders that, they argued, operated essentially as professional armies. Further, they complained about the papal privileges granted to the military orders that exempted them from diocesan assessments, the tithe, and other Church and secular taxes. The Hospitallers even claimed exemption from royal road tolls and the right to be judged solely by the pope for any civil or religious transgressions. Royal authorities were also vexed by the order's practice of admitting lay people, usually wealthy supporters, who were able to avoid paying secular taxes because of their affiliated membership in the order.

These criticisms were echoed by many bishops across Europe, who were upset by the loss of revenue and their lack of authority over the Templars and the Knights of St. John. The complaints were so numerous and persistent (they often surfaced in popular culture with songs and poems that poked fun at the military orders) that Pope Alexander III was compelled to raise the issue at the Third Lateran Council in 1179. However, the many prelates who brought complaints to the Holy See were sorely disappointed when Alexander rejected the criticisms and confirmed the military orders' privileges. The early decades of the thirteenth century witnessed a continuation of this criticism, but as the century wore on, the complaints slowly receded in the face of the growing favorable reputations of the Hospitallers and the Templars.

Although open to criticism because of their privileges and wealth, the Hospitallers, unlike the Templars, were more than just military men. From its inception, the order held its work with the poor and sick to be a fundamental aspect of its religious charism. Frá Ugo completely dedicated himself to this work after his return from the Holy Land. His example may well have been sufficient, at least in Genoa and its environs, to offset the vocal criticisms of the military knights. Where they were seen as proud, avaricious, and elitist, Frá Ugo was known as a kind and humble servant of the poor. Frá Ugo served at San Giovanni di Prè for about three decades. It was there, daily serving the poor and sick, that his holiness thrived and his name came to be revered by the people of Genoa.

When Frá Ugo settled in Genoa after the Third Crusade, San Giovanni was already a well-respected hospital that was strongly supported by the contributions of wealthy Genoese. It is known, for example, that from 1205 to 1226, the hospital was among the top five charitable institutions in Genoa remembered with bequests in registered wills (Epstein 1996). Its reputation as a welcoming and efficient hospital and way station for pilgrims was further burnished as word of the kindness and holiness of Frá Ugo circulated through the politically unsettled Genoese Republic.

Frá Ugo managed to stay above the violent political factionalism of the late twelfth and early thirteenth centuries, which saw the leading families of Genoa (Della Voltas, De Turcas, Ventros, and Spinolas, to name a few) vying for control of the political system and the Republic's growing wealth. There is nothing in the chronicles that indicates that Frá Ugo was drawn into the fray even when in 1224 his birthplace and a vassal city to Genoa, Alessandria, rose up with other towns against Genoese rule. The conflict ended in a negotiated settlement, with Milan acting as the arbitrator (Epstein 1996). Frá Ugo, from a leading Alessandrian family but now a widely admired religious in Genoa, apparently steered clear of any controversy and concentrated on his ministry.

Frá Ugo quickly made his mark on the commandery and its hospital. Staff and patients alike noticed his humility and keen desire to personally minister to the many poor and sick who came through the hospital's doors. It was said by chroniclers that the people of Genoa were first and foremost struck by his "heroic love" and "abundant charity." He was seen by the Genoese as the guardian of Jesus's poor and the protector of the weak. At San Giovanni, he took into the hospital everyone in need, not only the sick and dying, but also the homeless, the destitute, the pilgrim, and the simple weary traveler. Everyone in Genoa and its environs soon became aware that any marginalized person could, even in the worst of times, count on Frá Ugo's seemingly boundless love and compassion.

Frá Ugo was not the sort of man to be contented simply with efficiently administering his commandery. He wanted to care for "his lords, the sick and poor" himself, with his own hands, and he did just that. Stories abounded of his daily tending to patients, washing their feet, cleaning their bodies, treating their wounds, all the while exposing himself to illness and infection. He would often prepare the bodies of the dead for burial and accompany them to their resting places. The people of Genoa knew that something beautiful and Christ-like was happening at San Giovanni under the young Hospitaller knight from Alessandria.

Apart from his heroic charity, Ugo was known for his humility and piety. He lived simply in the commandery in a small room with a wooden board for a bed. The room overlooked the hospital so that he could monitor patients, with the harbor of Genoa just beyond. He lived an ascetic life and fasted frequently, sometimes for long periods of time. He practiced mortification of the senses and body, which were acceptable medieval acts of piety, and he was recognized for his prayer life and spirituality. Although no writings of Frá Ugo exist, the chronicles say that hundreds of people experienced his spirituality and holiness firsthand. He is said to have made himself available at any time, day or night, to anyone coming to him with spiritual needs. He gave "consolation to those in anguish; counsel to those in doubt; and instruction to those in ignorance" (Persoglio 1878).

In time, word circulated of miracles and extraordinary feats performed by this quiet, unassuming Hospitaller brother both before and after his death. The chronicles attest to his consequent growing fame. When during a drought he saw washer women struggling to carry the laundry of the hospital's poor a long distance to find water, it is said that he caused a spring to gush forth from a nearby rock. From the perch of his room window, he apparently calmed a squall by making the sign of the cross and saved a galleon in distress. Acknowledging Frá Ugo's role in the rescue, the crew went en masse to thank him in person at San Giovanni. He cast out demons, cured the lame, and on more than one occasion, changed water into wine. Archbishop Ottone of Genoa (1203–1239) and many others witnessed his levitations at Mass at his reception of the Eucharist.

Well before he died, Frá Ugo Canefri had become a revered and popular figure throughout the region. In a turbulent time of war and factionalism, he brought peace, caring, and love to Genoa's people. His humility and holiness attracted a wide following during his lifetime and even more so in death, as his cult rapidly spread throughout Italy and beyond. He spent over thirty years at San Giovanni serving his lords, the poor and sick. Almost immediately after his death in 1233, Archbishop Ottone, with strong popular backing, began to press for his canonization.

At the time, the formal process of canonization, introduced by the popes in the mid-twelfth century was still not widely followed. The ancient custom of popular acclamation and investigation by the local bishop was still practiced in most locales. In the case of Frá Ugo, Pope Gregory IX (1227–1241), who was to canonize Francis of Assisi, Dominic, and Anthony of Padua, requested that the details of the Hospitaller's miracles be sent to him in Rome. It is said that the pope then delegated Archbishop Ottone to determine the suitability of Frá Ugo for sainthood. The people of Genoa, however, did not wait for the archbishop's favorable judgment. With witnessed miracles both before and after his death in mind, the Genoese almost immediately dubbed Frá

Ugo *Santo*, although the Order of Malta apparently referred to him as blessed until the seventeenth century.

In 1631, the Vatican officially confirmed what all of Italy had come to believe hundreds of years earlier: that Frá Ugo Canefri had indeed lived a heroic life of virtue and was worthy to be venerated as a saint of the Roman Church. The Vatican marked his feast day as October 19, but the Order of Malta and Frá Ugo's many followers had always celebrated his feast on the day of his death, October 8. In the order's missal, his feast day remains October 8.

Collect From the Missal of the Sovereign Military Order of Malta

O God, who gave power to St. Hugh (Ugo) to grant relief to the sick with the sign of the Cross, grant, we pray, that, imbued with the spirit of your love, we may serve you in our brothers and sisters who are ill. Through our Lord Jesus Christ, your Son, who lives and reigns with you in the unity of the Holy Spirit, one God, for ever and ever.

4

St. Nicasius of Palermo

Circa 1135–Circa 1187

Tradition says that Nicasius of Palermo (also known as "of Jerusalem" and "of Sicily") was born around 1135 in Sicily and died in the Holy Land around 1187, a martyr at the hand of Sultan Saladin. Nicasius is a problematic figure in the roster of Hospitaller saints. Medieval scholars have recently pointed out the lack of documentary evidence relating to Nicasius, with some suggesting that Nicasius may never have even existed. There is no doubt, however, that a cult of prayer grew up around a certain Nicasius, first in Sicily and then in all southern Italy, beginning sometime in the late twelfth century, but there are several significant problems with the traditional narrative of his life.

According to this traditional narrative, Nicasius was born, the youngest son, to the family of combined Arab and Norman nobility. His grandfather was said to have been the last Saracen Emir of Girgenti and Castrogiovanni who, defeated by Count Roger, converted with his entire family to Christianity. He was baptized in 1088 in the presence of Roger

51

by the bishop of Girgenti, taking the name Roger Camuto. Shortly thereafter, Count Roger bestowed on the new convert the fiefdom of Castle Burgio, and the family added de Burgio to its name.

Nicasius's father, Roberto Camuto de Burgio, was said to have been born around 1080 and died in 1143. He married a young Norman aristocrat, Aldegonda d'Alta Villa, and they had four sons. The family was also said to have been close to the Norman monarchs Roger II, William I, and William II. Two of the sons, the second born, Ferrandino, and the last born, Nicasius, entered the Order of St. John, but it is not certain where or when. In 1085, the Hospitaller master Roger des Moulins called upon the Knights of St. John to reinforce the Christian Kingdom of Jerusalem. Nicasius and Ferrandino apparently answered the call.

In the hagiographic accounts of the life of Nicasius, the brothers were taken captive on July 4, 1087 by Saladin's forces at the Battle of Hattin, a crushing defeat for the Christians. In the aftermath of this disaster, fifty-two fortified Christian towns were lost to the Saracens, as they had been left lightly guarded, with Christian manpower instead concentrated on the army facing Saladin. Jerusalem itself fell on October 2, 1187. The Christian state was reduced to a shell of its former self, its capital moved to Tyre, and its forces dramatically weakened. Two years later in 1089, the Third Crusade was launched in an attempt by Latin Christendom to regain its footing in the Holy Land.

In the meantime, the fate of Ferrandino at the Battle Hattin was unknown, but it was said that Nicasius was captured and brought before Saladin. Saladin purportedly offered

Nicasius his life if he would renounce his faith and convert to Islam. Nicasius stubbornly refused, and he was beheaded, along with over two hundred other Templar and Hospitaller knights. Later retellings of the story claim that the arch-bishop of Tyre personally carried the news to William II in Palermo, and the king was overcome with grief. Immediately thereafter, according to the hagiographers, Nicasius began to be venerated as a martyr in Palermo and Sicily.

In some ways, this is a classic medieval depiction of a saint: a young nobleman gives up everything to fight the infidels for control of the Holy Land, in which Christ walked. He is captured by the Saracens, refuses to renounce his faith, and is put to death. It is important to note that to be considered a true martyr, the individual had to die for the faith in a very direct way. Nicasius is shown as having faced Saladin him-self, holding fast to his religion despite certain death. Thus, he may be venerated as a martyr. However, the problem with all this is that the life of Nicasius, as told by hagiographers since the seventeenth century, is not supported by any cred-ible contemporary sources.

Prominent medievalists, such as Helen Nicholson, point out that there is no mention of Nicasius by any of the south-ern Italian or Sicilian chroniclers, either before or after his death. While the miracles and extraordinary acts of medieval saints were often written about by contemporaries, there is nothing in the chronicles about Nicasius's miracles. There does not appear to be any record of his traveling to the Holy Land, and the presumed dates for his birth make it highly unlikely that he would have gone to the East in 1185 when he would have been between forty-seven and fifty-two years old (Nicholson 1995).

The first documentation of Nicasius's life was not until the late seventeenth century, over four hundred years after his death. His life was briefly outlined in the Hospitaller Giacomo Bosio's 1622 history of the order's saints, *Le Imagini de'Beati e Santi della Sacra Religione*. One of the purposes of Bosio's work was to convince the post-Council of Trent Church that the order's early saints would have been able to withstand modern (seventeenth century) scrutiny. One may, therefore, assume a certain amount of embellishment in Bosio's accounts to fit the medieval saints into the Tridentine criteria. Even so, Bosio could offer no contemporary primary sources to support his rendition of the life of Nicasius. Historians, in fact, have pointed out (Nicholson 1995) that the only hint of Nicasius's existence were "images in the churches of Palermo" that identify him as a Hospitaller and indicate that he suffered from swollen glands.

The question of whether Nicasius existed must have continued to arise even after the publication of Bosio's manuscript in 1622. About one hundred years later in 1762, Vincenzo Venuti, a Sicilian priest, wrote a highly defensive biography of Nicasius, setting forth a series of arguments aimed at those who doubted Nicasius's existence. Here, for the first time, is a detailed discussion of Nicasius's lineage, supported by the illustration of a family tree, all without any corroborating evidence. Venuti recounts a meticulously detailed story of Nicasius's life, unlike anything previously written, and this subsequently became the source for all future devotional accounts of the saint's life.

Nicholson and other medievalists point out that Venuti relied on one contemporary source to "prove" the existence of Nicasius: a charter said to be issued by Emperor Frederick II on August 24, 1232. Yet most medievalists dismiss the charter as a forgery, while also pointing out that the chronicles of the Battle of Hattin make no mention of a Nicasius. Even the *Acta Santorum*, the eighteenth-century "definitive" compendium of saints and blesseds compiled by the Jesuits, makes no mention of a St. Nicasius of Palermo (Nicholson 1995).

All this is not to say that there was no St. Nicasius. It is highly likely that there was a person named Nicasius who was locally venerated in Sicily in the twelfth century. Images of the saint were in Trapani church by 1305, suggesting that a cult was developing in Sicily around a figure who was thought to be a knight of St. John, crusader and martyr. Nicasius was said to have "performed many miracles" in Bosio's and Verdutti's biographies, but there are no specific examples or "signature" miracles either in contemporary accounts or later treatments. Well after the twelfth century, he appears to have been associated with curing illnesses of the throat, but again no contemporary examples are given anywhere in writing—although he was credited with saving Caccano from plagues in 1575 and 1624. Still, the prayer cult to St. Nicasius continued to grow in southern Italy, primarily by oral tradition, even without the essentials of sainthood: a body for relics, a grave site to revere, and a set of relatively undisputed facts around his life.

Within two hundred years of his death, Nicasius was widely known throughout southern Italy and Sicily. One of the most important promoters of Nicasius's legend was the Cabrese family (the counts of Modica). This influential clan claimed St. Nicasius as an ancestor, and in 1407, the family held a great feast to celebrate the saint in Caccano, underscoring its right to Nicasius's spiritual legacy and its attendant prestige. Also promoting devotion to St. Nicasius was the Dominican priest Giovanni Liccio, who was born in Caccamo around 1400 and was himself beatified in 1753. Liccio founded a Dominican convent in Caccamo and was known as a miracle worker until his death at over one hundred years old. In his travels throughout the kingdom, he frequently promoted popular devotion to his fellow Caccamese, St. Nicasius, which must have certainly helped the cult to prosper.

It is interesting to note there is no indication that the Order of St. John encouraged devotion to St. Nicasius or supported the expansion of his cult. Perhaps this was because of the order's long-standing aversion to singling out individual knights as martyrs, fearful of hurting morale and the sense of brotherly teamwork so necessary on the field of battle. Or perhaps the questions surrounding Nicasius's life were not sufficiently settled, from the order's point of view, to warrant the effort. In any case, the legend of St. Nicasius spread rapidly without the help of the Hospitallers (Nicholson 1995).

Tradition says that Nicasius was proclaimed a saint by consensus of the people not long after his death. In the sixteenth and seventeenth centuries, sensitive to Protestant criticisms of "saint-making," the Church sought to standardize further the rules and process for canonization. In some cases, it reviewed medieval saints to ensure that certain criteria had been met at the time of their popular acclamation. It appears as if Nicasius was part of that process. In 1625, Pope Urban VIII declared Nicasius servant of God, although he continued to be known as St. Nicasius. This may be why the *Acta Santorum* did not list St. Nicasius in its annals. That same year, St. Nicasius was declared the patron saint of Caccamo.

It is notable that a detailed depiction of Nicasius's life did not appear until the eighteenth century (Venuti 1762). This work, written to defend the existence of Nicasius, offered, for apparently the first time, a whole new set of "facts" and details about Nicasius's life without any evidence of their accuracy. Nonetheless, in ensuing centuries, hagiographers and others repeated this Venuti version of Nicasius's life in numerous and often brief written reflections on the saint. In a sense, Venuti's set of unverifiable details became "true" through constant repetition.

In the end, however, the accuracy of past accounts of St. Nicasius's life may make little difference—except in the valid interest of historical truth. With some degree of confidence, we can reasonably posit that a knight named Nicasius did exist, probably from Caccamo, who likely went off to the Holy Land in around 1185. He was, according to the early images, a holy knight of Christ. However, there must have been some question as to whether he was a knight of St. John because Venuti had to address this subject in his hagiography written centuries after Nicasius's death.

This knight died in the Holy land, not implausibly as one of the over two hundred captured knights of the military orders beheaded by Saladin. He was a martyr for the Faith, and his remains were not returned to Italy. By 1305, his legend had grown sufficiently that an altar was built to venerate him, and his images adorned at least one other church in the region. It is reasonable to assume that miracles, perhaps the curing of throat diseases, were attributed to him by the populace. He was acclaimed a saint by the people and the local bishop. In the mid-fifteenth century, his cult of prayer was promoted by a popular Dominican preacher throughout southern Italy. In the seventeenth century, he was recognized under the new canonization process as worthy of veneration.

This is all that can be said of St. Nicasius. Tradition tells of his heroic courage and faithfulness to the cross, his willingness to give his life for Christ, his role as protector and healer of the people of southern Italy. Somehow, the people's collective memory of St. Nicasius passed from generation to generation by oral tradition and kept the veneration of this saint alive for generations. Pope Urban gave Vatican affirmation of Nicasius's holiness in 1625, but this was a fact that the people of southern Italy had recognized for centuries.

The impact that St. Nicasius had after his death upon Sicily and beyond almost 840 years ago still reverberates today. At first, primarily a local saint, Nicasius remains faithfully venerated in Italy, especially Sicily, and in the Order of Malta. Because so little is known of Nicasius, perhaps it is best to view him through the eyes of the people of twelfth-century Sicily: a military man from the town of Caccamo, a martyr for the Faith, a healer of the people after his death, and a knight of St. John of Jerusalem.

The feast day of St. Nicarius is July 1.

Collect From the Missal of the Sovereign Military Order of Malta

O God, who gladdens us each year with the memorial of your Martyr, Saint Nicasius, grant that, through his example and intercession, all the members of our Order may continually grow in faith and hold fast to you with all their heart. Through our Lord Jesus Christ, your Son, who lives and reigns with you in the unity of the Holy Spirit, one God, forever and ever. Amen.

Blessed Gerard Mecatti
of Villamagna

Circa 1174–Circa 1242

Blessed Gerard Mecatti, also known as Gerard of Villa-magna, presents medievalists with several difficulties when it comes to determining the basic facts about his life. According to traditional hagiography, he was born in Villa-magna, a town not far from Florence, in or around the year 1174. It is generally accepted that he died around 1242.

Like Blessed Gerland, little is known of Gerard's child-hood or youth, as there appears to be no documentary evi-dence or mention of him in any chronicles. However, even if primary sources supporting the hagiographic details of his life are absent, there does appear to be proof that he at least existed. This proof comes in the form of incunabulum, a manuscript published in 1320 in Florence by Pacino de Bonaguida. It is a small book with thirty-eight illuminated pages. This may well be the earliest reference to Gerard's life thus far discovered.

The book, held at the Morgan Library and Museum in New York City, is entitled *Scenes from the Life of Christ and the Life of Blessed Gerard of Villamagna* (The Morgan, MS M.643 Vita Christi, Curatorial Notes, 1948). The images, most of which are depictions of the life of Christ, include five illustrations highlighting the life of Blessed Gerard. These portrayed Gerard distributing food, preaching, praying, and begging. The fifth image shows the body of Gerard tucked into a nook high above the ground in an elm tree. Tradition says that the town officials decided to place Gerard's casket in the tree to keep people from disturbing it by demanding, or helping themselves to, Gerard's remains in order to secure the sought-after relics of this holy man.

Initially in 1932, the saint in the book was misidentified by Italian scholar Umberto Noli, who believed him to be St. Octavianus, a fifth century figure who was martyred by the Vandals. This error was corrected in 1948 when scholars recognized Blessed Gerard of Villamagna as the saint depicted in the book. This is significant because the book was published in 1320, only about seventy-eight years after the consensus date of Gerard's death. His death has also been put by some hagiographers at 1277 which, if the date were to be accepted, would indicate that the book appeared just forty-three years after his demise. In any case, the existence of the images in this early thirteenth-century manuscript strongly suggest that although verified facts concerning his life may not exist, Gerard himself certainly did.

Setting aside the question of Gerard's existence, the fact remains that there is no mention of him in any chronicles or documents yet discovered. One of the concerns of medievalists is that Gerard died in the mid-thirteenth century, but nothing was written about him until 1551 when a local parish priest penned a hagiography of him. The hagiography included hitherto unknown details about Gerard's life without any references to sources. This portrayal of Gerard rested entirely upon oral tradition. Later, the *Acta Santorum* made no mention of Gerard's belonging to the Order of St. John. Instead, it described him simply as a Third Order Franciscan.

The 1551 hagiography, the 1662 hagiography of Giacomo Bosio on the saints of the order, and the scholarly work of the late seventeenth-century Bollandists are the only sources that exist concerning the life of Gerard. One must, therefore, assume that most of the details recounted century and century about Gerard have their origins in oral tradition. It is also possible to see in the writings about him some of the usual stratagems used by medieval and early modern hagiographers to demonstrate saintliness. Hence, there are historians who are inclined to term Gerard as "half legendary" and possibly an amalgam of several individuals (Nicholson 1990). This does not mean, however, that all the specifics about Gerard's life are suspect.

The traditional hagiographies say that Gerard was born into a family of modest means. His parents were peasants who worked the land and managed the estate of a wealthy family living in the city of Florence. Hagiographers normally took liberties in making saints of humble origins into scions of aristocratic families. In this case, however, Gerard's lowly social status was not covered over but rather treated quite openly in the literature. This suggests that Gerard may well have come from a farming family, although in truth this is entirely speculative.

At age twelve, Gerard lost his parents, and the noble Folci family took the boy into their own home and taught him to live a pious and Christian life. When Gerard was about sixteen years old, he was said to have been asked by a knight of St. John of Jerusalem to accompany him, probably as a squire, to the Holy Land on the Third Crusade (1189–1192). In the Holy Land, the knight and Gerard were said to have endured "many sufferings, including imprisonment." After the death of his noble protector, the young Gerard returned to Florence. There is, of course, no evidence to support these details, but the story did serve the purpose of making a connection between Gerard and the Order of St. John.

Back at home, tradition continues, Gerard began to live the life of a hermit. For twelve years, he lived in a small cabin near Villamagna, praying and fasting. His connection to the Holy Land and the Order of St. John was renewed when another unnamed knight sought him out to accompany him on the Fourth Crusade (1202–1204), infamous for its sacking of Christian Constantinople and failure to recapture Jerusalem. Gerard was said to have traveled by ship to the Holy Land and to have miraculously ensured a victory at sea against a superior Muslim force. The hagiographies do not say if Gerard was involved in the siege of Constantinople or if he was part of the small contingent of crusaders under Renard II of Dampierre, who fought, with minimal success, in the Holy Land while the bulk of the crusading force was sacking the capital of Christian Byzantium.

Tradition says that Gerard stayed in the Holy Land for seven years, tending the poor and sick. Some hagiographers place him in Jerusalem, which is impossible, since at that time the city was under the control of the Saracens. Nevertheless, while he was in the Holy Land, he was apparently invited to join the Order of St. John as a serving brother, a position held by commoners doing tasks such as carpentry, husbandry, and other skilled manual labor. All appeared to be going well, and word of Gerard's sanctity spread among the people. The hagiographers contend, however, that Gerard's humility was so offended by the people's admiration that he asked to be transferred back to Italy.

Once back home, he apparently felt the need to set aside all worldly distractions in favor of life as a hermit. So, as the story goes, he "withdrew into a wretched hovel . . . and became a hermit." Popular belief tells us that Gerard received from the "stigmatized hands of Saint Francis himself" the habit of the Friars Minor. Hagiographies, written three hundred to four hundred years later, argue that, despite the favor shown by St. Francis, Gerard did not leave the Order of St. John. Instead, he "wore the habits of both Religions one over the other." Hagiographers say that he combined the life of a Franciscan with that of a Hospitaller, which, given the immense differences between the two orders, would have been a miracle in and of itself. He apparently reconciled living the life of a secluded hermit with actively working to serve the sick and the poor, and he balanced his dedication to prayer and penance with his frequent preaching, counseling, and begging.

The *Vita Christi* manuscript's images do support some of the traditional stories about Gerard: his collecting alms for the poor (MS M.643 fol. 18v), giving alms to the poor (MS M.643 fol. 18r), praying and preaching (MS M.643 fol. 19r), and resting after his death in a coffin high above the ground in the branches of an elm tree (MS M.643 fol. 19v). The latter depiction is unique to the stories around Gerard of Villamagna. On the other hand, Gerard is shown in all five folios in the distinct brown garb of a Franciscan. There is no evidence that he wore both the habits of the Hospitallers and that of the Franciscans, or even an eight-pointed white cross on his Franciscan habit, as has been suggested by the hagiographers. This would seem to indicate that the *Acta Santorum* was correct in asserting that Blessed Gerard was probably a Franciscan.

From the mid-sixteenth century on, hagiographies continued to provide their readers with unsubstantiated details of Gerard's life. He helped St. Philip Benisi establish a confraternity in honor of Our Lady. He visited weekly three different churches situated very far apart. He prayed without ceasing for others and himself. He wore a hair shirt, scourged himself, and practiced other forms of self-flagellation. He was a reclusive hermit known to his contemporaries as the Antony or Hilarion (the great desert fathers) of his age; yet, at the same time, he was out and among the people, preaching and teaching. His charity and almsgiving was expansive.

His advice was sought after by hundreds of people. He walked on his knees three miles every night. He made cherries sprout in the winter when he was mortally ill and wanted to eat something. He foretold the date of his death

(May 13, 1254), and many miracles occurred at his tomb. On the site of his small hermitage, a church was built that today houses his body. All this was in addition to his life as a serving brother in the Order of St. John. Given the sheer immensity of this activity, historians can be forgiven if they speculate that the hagiographic treatments of Gerard were a compendium of several holy men's lives and not the story of one man (Nicholson 1990).

Despite confusion about the details of Gerard's life, there is little reason to deny the existence of a holy man by that name who lived in Villamagna in the thirteenth century. The fact that images of Gerard of Villamagna appeared in a 1320 book on the life of Christ published in Florence indicates the high regard in which this Gerard was held by the local population. In fact, if Gerard did not exist, the people of the Florentine environs would have likely denounced the *Vita Christi* as fraudulent for creating a false saint.

The highlights of Gerard's life are illustrated in the book, and from these images, it appears that he was perceived not as a Hospitaller but as a Franciscan focused on helping and preaching to the poor. There is no reference to the Hospitallers, no eight-pointed cross on his brown Franciscan habit, and no indication that the saint allegedly did two tours of duty in two separate Crusades, or that he was a serving brother in the Order of St. John. It is also unlikely that a Hospitaller serving brother would have been permitted to live a hermit's life, cut off from the order, its activities, and its commanderies.

Leaving aside his likely apocryphal life as a Hospitaller serving brother, Gerard clearly made a significant impact on the people of Villamagna. Already in 1320, only seventy-eight years after his purported 1242 death, he was considered a saint and worthy of being included in a book on the life of Christ. His life as a hermit, care for the poor, and miraculous works summed up the people's firsthand experience of this holy man. How and why he was eventually co-opted into the Hospitallers' roster of saints remains unclear. It does not appear as if the order made any effort to advance the cause for his sainthood. It can only be said that sometime between 1320 and 1622, Gerard was given a Hospitaller pedigree by hagiographers and that, consequently, today he is identified with both the Order of Malta and the Franciscans.

Gerard of Villamagna was a holy man who served the sick and poor and lived a personally ascetic life that was full of humility, piety, and compassion for the poor. Perhaps he was inspired by the charisms of the Order of St. John, but it is far more likely that he was inflamed by Franciscan values and the example of St. Francis of Assisi. The people's patient and faithful veneration of Gerard was finally recognized in 1833, almost six hundred years after his death, when he was beatified by Pope Gregory XVI. The inhabitants of Villamagna had an extraordinary devotion to Gerard, considering him a true saint long before Pope Gregory deemed him blessed.

His feast day is celebrated by the Order of Malta on May 18 and by the Franciscans on May 23.

Collect From the Missal of the Sovereign Military Order of Malta

O God, who called Blessed Gerard, like your own son, to intense striving in the wilderness, strengthen us by penance and prayer and make us fitter for our Christian duties. We ask this through our Lord Jesus Christ your Son, who lives and reigns with you and the Holy Spirit, one God for ever and ever. Amen.

6

Blessed Gerland of Germany

Died Circa 1242

G erland of Germany is a medieval saint who presents
certain challenges to the biographer, since there are virtually no contemporaneous records of his life. He is said to
have died around 1242 after a life of service as a professed
knight in the Order of Malta.

Gerland's hagiographers have never been able to agree on
the date or place of his birth. Some said Germany, others
Poland, and still others Bologna. In some accounts, he was
said to have died in or around 1242, while other accounts
put the year of his birth at 1240. Because there is a general
hagiographic consensus, this monograph will refer to Gerland as "of Germany" and assume that his death occurred
sometime around 1242.

There are no documents or clues to Gerland's early life,
which is not surprising since even the country of his birth
remains uncertain. Nothing is known of his lineage, childhood, or education. For specifics on his adult life, one must
look to Giacomo Bosio's 1622 work on the lives of the

Hospitaller saints entitled *Le Imagini de' Beati Santi della Sacra Religione*. However, reliance on Bosio's information is risky indeed since he offers almost no evidence for the detailed portrait that he paints of Gerland's life.

Bosio, who was a member of the order, wrote in the seventeenth century, almost sixty years after the Council of Trent tightened the procedures for declaring sainthood. The order had many saints and blesseds who were beatified under the more lax medieval customs. Bosio intended to produce a volume that would justify the canonizations of the order's medieval saints by demonstrating that they could withstand the scrutiny of the new process. He produced detailed hagiographies, but they were far from accurate. When he ran into a dearth of documents, he essentially made up the details. In the case of Gerland, Bosio readily admitted that nothing was known of his origins or childhood, but he related a great deal of unsubstantiated information about his adult life.

In Bosio's telling, Gerland arrived from Jerusalem on the island of Sicily in the early thirteenth century, sent by the master of the Knights of St. John. His assignment was to supervise the order's property in the province of Catania, which was then under the rule of the German Swabian dynasty, the Hohenstaufens. He was also instructed to represent the order at the court of the celebrated and controversial Emperor Frederick II in Palermo.

By the beginning of the thirteenth century, the Order of St. John, commonly known as the Hospitallers, was recognized as a formidable crusading military force and a stabilizing influence in the Christian Kingdom of Jerusalem. The order's military prowess and its extensive charitable work among the sick and poor resulted in hundreds of gifts of landed estates from admiring European monarchs and nobility. It was not uncommon to send professed knights to live in these estates or commanderies to manage them and supply the convent in Jerusalem with a portion of the estates' revenues. It is said that Gerland was sent to Sicily in that role.

The emperor's court in Palermo was known by contemporaries not only for its splendor and opulence but also as an intellectual meeting ground for Greek, Latin, and Arab cultures. As the representative of the master of the Order of St. John, Gerland apparently dressed in magnificent finery, commensurate with his rank and role. Bosio says that beneath the fine clothes, Gerland wore a hair shirt. He fasted rigorously and periodically scourged himself—all penitential practices often employed by the zealous at the time.

It was said that Gerland had a reputation for humility and holiness and that he was known for his care of the poor and sick. He was supposed to have given liberally to the poor, helped anyone in need, and rushed to the aid of those suffering injustice and abandonment, regardless of religion. He provided an edifying example to the members of the emperor's court, but the hagiographers lament that the courtiers did not heed the lessons that he offered them.

He is said to have died in 1242, and the poor of Caltagirone mourned him deeply. He was buried outside the city walls, and his tomb was apparently the site of many miracles and cures. However, sometime between 1242 and 1327, in a span of only eighty-five years, the grave site of Gerland was lost. In 1327, a devout Hospitaller knight in Syracuse had a dream in which Constantine appeared to him and pointed out the location of Gerland's grave. The knight and his confreres went to the spot, which was a ruined church, and discovered Gerland's body and the surrounding air filled with a sweet fragrance.

Gerland's remains were brought to the Basilica di San Giacomo Maggiore, and his bones were cleaned and washed in wine. In the ensuing weeks, until July 20, 1327, one hundred miraculous cures were attributed to drinking the wine that washed his bones. These healings were apparently witnessed by many Caltagirone officials. It is said that he was pronounced a saint sometime in the mid-fourteenth century by popular acclamation and approval of the local bishop.

Certainly, the story of Gerland is inspirational and instructive: an urbane courtier and professed knight, living outside the convent, and an edifying figure, serving the sick and the poor. In short, he was a man able to bridge his secular life with his religious vocation, at ease with both royalty and peasants alike. Similar to many medieval saints, miracles were said to have occurred at his tomb, which was inexplicably lost, and then more miracles again after it was rediscovered some eighty-five years after his death.

Medievalists generally cast a jaundiced eye upon Bosio's rendition of the life of Gerland. First, Bosio cites no documents to support his narrative. He bases his conclusion that Gerland was a Hospitaller solely on the existence of an anonymous portrait done in the 1580s of Blessed Gerland in the order's black habit with the eight-pointed white cross (Nicholson 1990). Thus far, no record of Gerland joining the order has surfaced, although this would not be unusual given the spotty record keeping of the thirteenth century. Still, it has been determined that the ruins of the church which housed the tomb of a knight (said to be Gerland) was a Templar church until 1310, just two years prior to the pope's suppression of the Templar Order. Hagiographers generally agreed that Gerland died around 1244. It is highly improbable that he, as a Hospitaller, would have been entombed in a Templar church. This would indicate that the knight, who was discovered in 1327 in the ruins of the church, was a Templar rather than Hospitaller (Licence 2005).

Furthermore, other historians point out that the region of Sicily in which the church ruins were located was not an area of Hospitaller activity. The order was not known to have owned any property nor had any commanderies around Caltagirone. From 1312, the year the Templars were suppressed, to 1327, the year of the miraculous discovery of Gerland's tomb, the Hospitallers were seeking to inherit Temple properties throughout Europe. Proclaiming an unknown, newly discovered, miracle-working knight as a Hospitaller strengthened this claim in Sicily. Also, one medievalist points out that had the people of Caltagirone proposed a Templar for sainthood, it was not likely that the pope would have approved. The Temple had just been suppressed by the Avignon pope, who was subject to French influence, and it was the French king who had led the effort to eliminate the Templars (Nicholson 1990).

Finally, it is difficult to reconcile the assertion that Gerland's first tomb was the site of remarkable miracles with the fact that his resting place was "lost" in the course of some eighty-three years from his death to his rediscovery. Given the intensity of medieval devotion to local saints, it is unlikely that the people of Caltagirone would have suddenly lost their way to such a benefactor's tomb. It is true that the kingdom was thrown into a political turmoil upon the death of Frederick in 1250. A struggle ensued, which saw the Hohenstaufens battle the House of Anjou for the crown, and it did not end until 1302.

Still, even this disruption is an unconvincing explanation for "misplacing" the site of so many apparent miracles. More plausible, as some medievalists suggest, is that an unknown knight was discovered in the ruins of the Templar church outside the town walls in 1327. The authorities, aware of the fate of the Templars and knowing that they could not advance the cause of a member of that disgraced order, claimed that the knight was a Hospitaller.

This is not to say that miracles did not occur when the sick drank the wine that had washed his bones or that miraculous happenings did not continue at his new resting place in the basilica. The oral tradition seems to indicate that the Caltagirone authorities witnessed many of these works of wonder. Also at some point, well after 1327, the local bishop was sufficiently persuaded of this knight's holiness and reputation as a worker of miracles to raise him to sainthood. Although some scholars are highly skeptical that Gerland ever existed (Licence 2005; Demurger 2005), it seems likely that there was an unidentified knight, given the name Gerland, whose grave was discovered in 1327. His relics may well have spawned miracles after 1327, and he was beatified at the urging of the people of Caltagirone. However, it is evident that little more can be said with confidence about his life.

It cannot be shown that this Gerland was a member of the order, nor can it be said that he was the order's representative to the court of Frederick II. Certainly, the hagiographies of Giovanni Bosio and Francois Ducand-Bourget are not helpful, the former having concocted the original misinformation about Gerland and the latter perpetuating these unsubstantiated claims hundreds of years later. Filling biographical blanks with fabricated details cannot be justified by pious claims that the goal of hagiographies is to inspire devotion to the saints, for genuine devotion cannot be based on falsehood.

Yet the truth about Blessed Gerland, as far as it can be surmised, need not be an impediment to admiration or veneration. This knight existed, probably in the thirteenth century. His grave was discovered among the ruins of a Templar church around 1327. He was then given a name Gerland and called a Hospitaller. The common people attested to miraculous works that came about through his intercession, and a bishop eventually deemed him blessed.

Somehow and for some reason, the people of fourteenth-century Sicily, who discovered his tomb, experienced in this unknown knight a degree of holiness. In their simple faith, they petitioned him to intercede with heaven on their behalf, and he apparently did so to their satisfaction. It did not matter to them if he were born in Poland or Germany, a Templar or Hospitaller, or a noble at the imperial court or a poor itinerant knight. Though they did not know him in life, they asked their bishop to recognize the heroic virtue of their Blessed Gerland, and he did so some one hundred years after his resting place was discovered.

The Order of St. John claimed this unknown knight as its own almost seven hundred years ago. To this day, he remains a member of the order's litany of saints. Blessed Gerland's feast day is celebrated on June 19.

Collect From the Missal of the Sovereign Military Order of Malta

Lord God, who led Blessed Gerland from the northern lands into Sicily and inspired him to exchange the armor of our Order for sackcloth, mercifully enkindle our zeal, so that our manner of life will always aim at perfection. Through our Lord Jesus Christ, your Son, who lives and reigns with you in the unity of the Holy Spirit, one God forever and ever.

7

Blessed Peter Pattarini of Imola

Circa 1250–1320

Blessed Peter of Imola was born sometime in the mid-thirteenth century to the noble Pattarini family, the rulers of the Linasio region, northwest of Florence. He died in Florence on October 5, 1320.

There is little known of the early life of Peter Pattarini. He apparently grew up as a typical young aristocrat in the late thirteenth century. His family was allied to the Ghibelline political faction, which supported the Holy Roman emperor in the political and territorial conflicts with the papacy. The struggle between the emperor and the pope had its roots in the rivalry between two German factions vying for the dignity of Holy Roman emperor: the Hohenstaufens and the House of Welf, the rulers of Bavaria. From these two families came the terms *Ghibellines* (derived from the Hohenstaufen castle of Wibellingen) and *Guelfs* (derived from the House of Welf). In short, the former fought against the expansion of papal temporal power and the latter against the spread of German influence in Italy.

About the time of the birth of Peter Pattarini in 1250, the Hohenstaufen emperor, Frederick II, died after waging decades of war in Italy against the papacy and its allies. His son, Conrad IV, ruled for only four years, and from 1254 to 1273, there was no effective Holy Roman emperor. The Guelfs and Ghibellines continued to struggle in northern Italy even beyond 1268 when the last male in the Hohenstaufen dynasty, Conradin, was executed by the Guelf king Charles I of Naples.

The execution of Conradin did not, however, completely end the rivalry between the two factions, especially in the region of Florence, where the Pattarinis were local landed aristocrats. The Tuscan Ghibellines were finally defeated at the battle of Campaldino in 1268 when Peter of Imola would have just been entering young manhood, but the unrest between the pro-German and pro-papacy factions persisted in local clashes. The Guelfs themselves fell into disagreement in Florence, splitting into Black and White factions, the Blacks continuing to support papal power and the Whites opposing any extension of the pope's territories and influence. By 1302, the Black Guelfs had ousted the Whites from Florence, whom they accused of being secret Ghibellines.

In 1325, Guelph Bologna and Ghibelline Modena fought a brief war that ended in defeat for the Guelfs and a resurgence of the Ghibelline influence in the region. Although Pope Benedict XII attempted to suppress the use of the monikors Guelph and Ghibelline, the struggle between these two sides continued in northern Italy well beyond the death of Peter of Imola in 1320. Thus, the backdrop for the life of Blessed Peter was this intense political struggle, which waxed and waned during his life, and this may help to shed some light on his person.

It may safely be said that Blessed Peter was a highly regarded lawyer and judge in the region. The documents from Imola during the latter part of the thirteenth century cite a certain "lawyer and jurist," Peter Pattarini, as practicing law in Imola. His name is also apparently found in a 1289 index of city magistrates, when he would have been around thirty-nine years old. Further documentation names him as the principal mediator in a 1299 peace treaty between warring Guelf and Ghibelline factions in Emilia Romagna. Blessed Peter apparently remained in Imola until 1311, as there are documents that place his location in that city. It is known that in 1310, Emperor Henry VII visited Italy, and one year later the Ghibellines were driven out of Romagna by the Guelfs. This action apparently affected even a highly respected jurist as Peter Pattarini, and he left for Florence in 1311 at the approximate age of sixty-one.

In Florence, Blessed Peter did not exactly find a haven for nobles or Ghibellines. The city had enacted the Ordinances of Justice in 1293 that barred aristocracy from holding office, reserving that right to members of the guilds. The White Guelfs had been exiled from the city, tainted with the charge of secretly allying with the still active, if chastened, Ghibelline strongholds. In his early sixties and a well-known Imolese jurist from a prominent noble Ghibelline family, Peter could have hardly imagined that he would simply continue his career in Florence without missing a beat. In fact, his arrival in Florence in 1311 marked the beginning of a new life for Blessed Peter.

A refugee in Florence and likely unable to practice his profession, Peter began to involve himself in volunteer work for the poor in a hospital operated by the Order of St. John of Jerusalem (Order of Malta). He quickly became interested in the order and took his vows as a professed knight around 1312. His long and distinguished secular career was put to good use by the order, whose superiors saw the value of his administrative and legal background. He was named grand prior of Rome and spent several years in Rome before returning to Florence to reside in the Commandery of St. James in Campo Corbellini. He continued his focus on the poor and sick, visiting them in their homes and caring for their needs.

Blessed Peter Pattarini died on October 5, 1320, around the age of seventy. He is a telling example of the efficacy of a late vocation, a man of the secular world who probably spent less than ten years in religious life, but he so struck the people of Florence that he was acclaimed a saint after working among them for only a brief period. With his life, he demonstrated that late vocations and secular experience can indeed lead one to sanctity. Blessed Peter spent about sixty-one of his seventy years outside the Order of St. John of Jerusalem, but today he is venerated as one of the order's holiest members in its history.

Blessed Peter is buried in the Church of St. James in the Campo Corbolini. The Church of St. James, founded on May 3, 1206, is colloquially called the Church of Gates (San Iacopo dei Cancelli) in recognition of the gates present since ancient times. The church passed to the Knights of Malta after the original proprietors, the Knights Templar, ceased to exist in 1312.

Although there are very likely unrecorded instances of miracles after his death (which would have led to the popular acclamation of his sainthood), there is one miracle ascribed to Blessed Peter that stands out for its unusual, and even macabre, nature. It is reported to have occurred in the Church of St. James where it is affirmed by witnesses that from his resting place, the saint's arm stilled a tottering ladder, thus saving the lives of workers laboring to decorate the church. After the miracle, the saving arm was detached from his body, and his remains were taken and laid under the altar of the Madonna in the Basilica of St. Lorenzo in Florence. After a flood of the Arno in 1557, the reliquary containing the arm of Blessed Peter was submerged for several days, yet the flesh and nails were said to have escaped all damage and are venerated to this day.

His feast day is celebrated on October 5.

Collect From the Missal of the Sovereign Military Order of Malta

O God, who gave blessed Peter, Prior of our Order, the gift of settling disputes, grant, we pray that through his intercession, that we may become peacemakers, and so be called children of God. Through our Lord Jesus Christ, your son, who lives and reigns with you in the unity of the Holy Spirit, one God, forever and ever.

8

St. Toscana of Verona

Circa 1280–Circa 1343

St. Toscana was born in a small town outside of the Italian city-state of Verona in the latter part of the thirteenth century. She entered the Order of St. John around 1318 and died around 1343.

Little is known of this early Hospitaller saint except that she was born in Zevio and spent much of her adult life in Verona. At the time of Toscana's birth, the "free commune" of Verona, which had been established in 1135, was a prosperous but conflict-torn city-state. For much of the twelfth and thirteenth centuries, the region was a battleground between the forces of the papacy (Guelfs) and those of the German Holy Roman emperors (Ghibellines). During Toscana's lifetime, Verona transitioned from an oligarchic quasi-democracy in which the leader, or podesta, was elected by the Great Council to a state dominated by Mastino I (Della Scala), who was assassinated in 1277, and his descendants.

Having consolidated political power in Verona, the successors of Mastino I concentrated on expanding the borders of Verona. Toscana's adult years were lived out in an environment marked by constant warfare and conflict between Verona and its neighboring states. In the first three decades of the fourteenth century, Verona brought under its control Padua, Treviso, Vicenza, Brescia, Parma, and Lucca. However, by 1340, just a few years before Toscana's death, Venice and Florence joined with other neighboring states to strip Verona of much of its territory, leaving only Vincenza as part of the free commune.

Although there are no documents that indicate Toscana was influenced by these events, it is impossible to think that she was oblivious to the world around her. Likely of noble birth, her family would have been compelled to takes sides in the struggle between the pope and the emperor, and she would have most certainly encountered many wounded veterans of the Veronese wars in her hospital work. However, unlike St. Catherine of Siena, there is nothing in the historical record that renders a clue as to the thoughts or views of Toscana on her times.

The earliest sources on Toscana's life appear to be two hagiographic vitas by Celso Dalle Falci, written in 1474, and Lodovico Moscardo, written in 1668. Although useful, these works present all the problems associated with the reconstruction of the lives of early medieval saints, since their purpose was to edify rather than to inform. In these accounts, Toscana is said to be of noble birth, beautiful and virtuous from infancy. These are standard descriptors given to medieval saints, particularly females.

This is not to say that some, or even all, of these descriptors do not apply to Toscana. However, for verification, there are only the hagiographers' works to rely upon, with little scholarship from modern medievalists to support them. Nevertheless, there are certain basic facts about Toscana that appear accurate: the general events of her life, her acceptance into the Order of St. John of Jerusalem, and the circumstances of her death.

Although her family name is unknown, Toscana was likely born into a family of minor nobility since contemporary accounts say that she was married to an aristocrat, Alberto Canoculi (Occhio di Cane). Some medieval scholars question the traditional dates of Toscana's birth and death, alleging that she may well have been born in 1100. They cite documents in the *Archivio dei Santi Apostoli* that refer to a Toscana from the noble family of Costanzio dei Crescenzi born in Zevio around that time. Still, until further research on this issue is undertaken, it seems prudent to accept the traditional years of Toscana's life (late thirteenth and early fourteenth centuries) and the fact that her surname remains unknown (Luttrell and Nicholson 2006).

The hagiographic sources place Toscana's marriage as having taken place in 1310 when, according to the traditional understanding of her birth date, she would have been around thirty or thirty-one years old, rather an advanced age for a first-time medieval bride. Even before marriage, Toscana spent considerable time caring for the poor and indigent in Zevio, and she was apparently well-known among the townspeople as a virtuous and caring young woman. Her marriage to Canoculi and subsequent move to nearby Verona did not lessen her desire to serve society's less fortunate. She is said to have remained chaste, her marriage to

Canoculi unconsummated. It does appear as if there were no children from the brief marriage, but it should be kept in mind that the assignation of virginity to late vocations was a frequent tool used by medieval hagiographers to heighten the sanctity of their subjects' lives.

Alberto Canoculi is said to have died four years after the marriage. If this is accurate, Toscana would have been around thirty-five years old. As a still relatively youthful noble woman of recognized virtue, she would have conceivably made a desirable match for an older, widowed aristocrat. However, Toscana showed no interest in a second marriage. She apparently lived alone for several years, continuing her service to the sick and poor by volunteering at the Order of St. John's Holy Sepulcher Hospital.

Around 1318, Toscana sought entrance into the Order of St. John. She sold her goods and was accepted into the order as a donat or conversa. Although not technically a vowed religious, she was given the right to wear the habit of the order and lived in a small cell in the community adjacent to Holy Sepulcher Hospital where she continued to work. Donats often came from noble families, promised to leave their wealth to the order, and had the right to fully enter the order at a time of their choosing.

It was around this time that Toscana began to be known in Verona for her extreme fasts. She is said to have "lived on bread and water with a little oil for feast days." Toscana is listed, along with the Hospitaller saint Ubaldesca, among the 261 medieval "holy anorexics" by scholars (Bell 1985) who have studied the history of anorexia. The extreme self-starvation exhibited by saintly medieval women reflected the drive for spiritual purity in the context of imitating Christ. Holy anorexics denied themselves all sustenance but the bare minimum necessary to survive.

Bell observes, "Towards others the holy girl is docile and uncomplaining, even servile, and yet in her spiritual world her accomplishments are magnificent." Through extreme fasting, a holy anorexic became the master of herself, the servant of God, but not of man, in control of her every feeling (Bell 1985).

Medieval society often did not know how to react to such holy women. It struggled to determine if this odd behavior came from God or the evil one. Most often, it concluded that the devil was the source of this strange activity. Yet when it was accompanied by a holy, virtuous life and miraculous events recognized by the community, these women became the objects of intense awe and devotion. Such was the case with Toscana, whose exemplary life of humble service to the poor was apparently combined with many miracles both before and after her death.

It appears that Toscana was known for her cures of many illnesses, very often healing people with severe and dangerous fevers. She herself suffered from frequent fevers, and it was said that she was particularly empathic to others who exhibited this malady. Her chastity was also held in high esteem by her contemporaries. In this regard, the following story of three would-be burglars and rapists was apparently often-told and well-known in Verona while Toscana was still alive.

It is said that sometime between her husband's death and her entrance into the Order of St. John, Toscana confronted three delinquents who broke into her house in the middle of the night. One after the other was struck down by divine intervention before they could harm Toscana. Distressed by the fact that her assailants died without the sacrament of Penance and moved by the despair of the delinquents' families, Toscana prayed that they would be restored to life and be permitted to make their confessions. Although the men were clearly dead, it was said that they were miraculously revived, made their confessions, and died again immediately afterward. Many public miracles were said to have taken place at Toscana's tomb, and within a few decades, the cult of Toscana began to grow in the region and beyond.

In 1474, Dalla Falci published his pamphlet on Toscana's life, furthering her fame. In 1500, the church attached to the order's hospital in Verona was named for St. Toscana. In 1600, an altar in the Zevio cathedral was dedicated to Toscana. In 1613, the local bishop, Alberto Valier arranged for some of Toscana's relics to be transmitted to Zevio. The transfer of the relics was accompanied by large crowds of devout citizenry and warmly welcomed by the faithful of Zevio. The saint was subsequently credited with saving the city from the plague, as well as from a severe drought. In 1684, some of Toscana's relics were sent to the island of Malta to rest in the Church of St. John, cementing her position as a "Hospitaller saint."

Although much about the life of St. Toscana is obscure, this much is known. She apparently lived a life of humility, charity, and love, and her virtues were widely recognized and admired by her contemporaries. She was held in awe for her severe fasting, which was seen by much of medieval society as a means for a select few holy women to become more Christ-like. The people of Verona and Zevio witnessed her numerous miracles both while she lived and after her death. A noble woman by birth, she ultimately gave up her wealth and property in exchange for a small room and inclusion in the community of St. John of Jerusalem. She worked every day in the order's hospital caring for the poor and sick, a task that most noble born religious women did not do.

Although Toscana lived some eight hundred or more years ago, her life of heroic virtue continues, especially in Verona and Italy, to inspire the enduring popularity of, and a genuine devotion to, this Hospitaller saint.

St. Toscana is buried in Verona in the church that bears her name. Her feast day is July 14.

Collect From the Missal of the Sovereign Military Order of Malta

O God, who, amid the turbulence of this world, were pleased to keep safe in marriage and widowhood your servant Saint Toscana, and wondrously made her outstanding in our Order for her charity to the poor, mercifully grant that, sincerely serving you by diligently imitating her, we may be pleasing to you by our faith and our works. Through our Lord Jesus Christ, your Son, who lives and reigns with you in the unity of the Holy Spirit, one God for ever and ever.

9

St. Fleur de Beaulieu

Died 1347

St. Fleur (also known as Flor) de Beaulieu was born around the latter part of the thirteenth century in Maurs, a town in south-central France. She died in 1347 at the Hospitaller Monastery of Beaulieu.

Little is known of Fleur's early years, there being considerable confusion about her birth date and her social standing. When in the seventeenth century the Jesuits Heribert Rosweyde and his researchers were preparing the *Acta Sanctorum*, a compendium of the lives of the saints, they came across one volume on Fleur written by Giocomo Bosio, the author of a hagiographic compendium on the saints of the Order of St. John of Jerusalem that was published in 1622. Bosio's work was rife with errors and exaggerations, and he took a good deal of license with the facts. His treatment of Fleur was no different than his overblown and factually-challenged descriptions of other medieval Hospitaller saints whose origins and lives may have been somewhat obscure, leaving Bosio's imagination to fill in the blanks.

In the case of St. Fleur, Bosio relied on a poorly translated (written in the local Quercy dialect) and partially destroyed vita by Fleur's confessor. It was written in the fourteenth century apparently by someone who knew Fleur, but it had been lost in the original by the time the Jesuits were compiling the *Acta Sanctorum* at the beginning of the eighteenth century. Essentially, Bosio's biography, with its references to the vita, was the principal source for information on the life of Fleur. The *Acta Sanctorum*, published in 1715, influenced the hagiographic writings on Fleur until the mid-twentieth century. Consequently, there are many apocryphal stories about Fleur still circulating to this day (L'Hermite-Leclercq 2006).

Traditionally, Fleur's birth date was said to be around 1309, but this is based on pure speculation. Documents place her in the Monastery of Beaulieu in 1327 (although she may well have entered earlier at the beginning of the fourteenth century), and there are references to her "long life." Since we know her death was in 1347 and her life was apparently long, most medievalists today put her birth in the late thirteenth century (circa 1287), making her around sixty when she died. There can be, however, no certainty given to any of these dates, except that of her death.

St. Fleur is also said to have been born of an aristocratic family, but there is no evidence of this at all. In fact, the manuscripts of the period cite her father's name, Pons of Corby, but medievalists can find no trace of a noble family of this name in the Maurs region. Assertions in later hagiographic writings traced nobility through her mother, but recent scholarship has debunked this as well. The complete lack of documents on this question leave her origins uncertain, although it remains unlikely that she came from an aristocratic family (L'Hermite-Leclerq 2006).

Fleur likely entered the monastery of the Hospitallers sometime immediately after 1298, when the monastery was granted official affiliation with the Order of St. John. Under its charter, the nuns had the right to elect their own superior and were only loosely attached to the nearby Priory of St. Giles, which housed the knights of St. John and their servants and retainers. The extent of this attachment appeared to be that the prior had the right of visitation, but little more. The charter also put a ceiling of thirty-nine as the maximum number of professed sisters permitted to reside at the community.

When Fleur entered the monastery, her confessor relates, she was disturbed by the level of luxury in which the nuns lived. This should have come as no surprise, however, since the Order of St. John's communities were well-known as being among the least restrictive and least demanding among medieval religious orders. Although she expressed concern about the excessive comforts, Fleur did not leave the order's monastery and seek out a more severe arrangement. She apparently adhered on her own to a more rigorous religious lifestyle than her community required. She practiced abstinence, fasted for long periods, deprived herself of sleep, and displayed an intense and demonstrative prayer life.

At first, her superiors and sisters did not know what to make of Fleur. She apparently did not work with the poor and sick (it is questionable if any of the sisters at Beaulieu did so), but from the outset, her religious life was centered on reciting the

Divine Office, the Eucharist, prayer, and meditation. She ran about the convent with spastic movements, gyrating her body and looking up to heaven. She had the gift of tears, breaking out in frequent sobs of devotion. Her confessor says that many thought of Fleur as mad and unhinged.

One medieval scholar described Fleur's behavior in the convent: "She was an eccentric mystic whose experiences of hovering during Mass and being pregnant with the cross upset the day-to-day communal life at Beaulieu" (Bom 2012). "Pregnant with the cross" refers to Fleur's unusual stigmata. She is said to have internalized the cross so that every Friday, blood gushed from her side and mouth, not from the traditional five wounds. Her previous torment and trials were so intense that contemporaries believed this internalizing of Christ's passion was the cause of the stigmata.

At some point, however, she is said to have begun to receive consolations, as Christ appeared to her over the course of several months. Once consoled, she continued to experience ecstasies (one lasting from November 1 to 22 during which she ate and drank nothing), levitations, and visions. Fleur was said to be able to predict the future and read the innermost secrets of people's hearts. Angels played a major role in her ecstasies and visions, much more so than for other contemporary saints. In short, Fleur, in a relatively brief period, took her place beside the great medieval mystics, and over time, the nuns of Beaulieu's attitudes changed from skepticism and disdain to awe and respect.

L'Hermite-Leclercq relates a story written down by Fleur's confessor, an avid believer in her sanctity. He met a man on the road who remarked to him, "If Christ had two mothers,

Fleur would have been the second." High praise indeed from a fourteenth-century believer. No doubt the fame of Fleur as a mystic and holy woman, a worker of miracles, had spread widely in southeastern France, and well before her death in 1347, she was already considered a holy and saintly woman by the people.

According to certain manuscripts, Fleur's miracles, which were apparently numerous and well publicized, began while she was still alive and continued for approximately two centuries after her death. There is documentation recording sixty-nine healings, including curing epilepsy (then known as St. Namphase's evil), blindness, deafness, paralysis, plague, and other infirmities. Interestingly, women were the beneficiaries of many of her cures. Many miracles (twenty-seven) occurred in the town of Beaulieu itself, but scores of others were spread around the region (L'Hermite-Leclercq 2006).

Although indisputably a nun in the Order of St. John, Fleur's life as a religious did not follow the normal course of some Hospitaller women. There is no indication that she ever worked with the poor or sick in the nearby hospital. Almost immediately after entering the monastery, Fleur became focused on her prayer life and the recitation of the Divine Office. As her spiritual torments surrounded her and eventually gave way to consolations, her life became one focused entirely on prayer and miracles. There is apparently no record of St. Fleur ministering to the poor or working in any of the order's hospitals.

Although during her lifetime she became famous for her holiness and miraculous healings throughout south-central France, the French commanderies of the order displayed little interest in her mysticism and miracles. As one medievalist points out, Fleur performed no miracles after her death at Rhodes or Cyprus nor did she cure any members of the order (L'Hermite-Leclercq 2006). The order, in turn, appears not to have taken up her cause for sainthood, a fact that is true for almost all the order's beatified and canonized members. Instead of the order, the local population witnessed to Fleur's life of virtue and grace and publicly acclaimed her holiness, which, in time, was confirmed by the bishop of Cahors.

Although one cannot point to any specific charisms of the order that inflamed the virtue of St. Fleur, she was nevertheless a Hospitaller sister for her entire religious life. Her impact on her contemporaries was immense, and her goodness and holiness were witnessed by hundreds of people in the Diocese of Cahors and surrounding areas. In her early years, her eccentric behavior raised suspicions and doubts within the monastery, but these were overcome as her consolations and mystical experiences ultimately altered the way people saw her.

For a medieval saint, the documentation of her many miracles is as unusual as it is impressive. Her miraculous cures, devotion to prayer, and witnessed ecstasies had a significant impact on her contemporaries who clamored for her sainthood upon her death. She is venerated as the patron of converts, single women, and the abandoned. Her relics remain in the Diocese of Cahors where she died at Beaulieu in 1347. Her feast day is celebrated on June 12.

Collect From the Missal of the Sovereign Military Order of Malta

Almighty and merciful God, who willed that Saint Fleur, suffused with the dew of heavenly grace, should blossom with the beauty of virginity and charity in the Order of St. John of Jerusalem, grant, we pray, that by her example we may merit to grow continually in your love, who lives and reigns with you in the unity of the Holy Spirit, one God, forever and ever.

10

St. Nuno Alvarez Pereira

1360–1431

St. Nuno Alvarez Pereira, also known as the Holy Constable and St. Nuno of St. Mary, was born in 1360, most
probably at Cernache do Bomjardim in central Portugal. He
died in 1431 in Lisbon in the Carmelite convent after a celebrated military career and a widely admired religious life.
He is considered one of Portugal's most important historical
figures.

Nuno Alvarez Pereira, the seventh Count of Barcelos,
third Count of Ourem, and second Count of Arraiolos, was
born on June 24, 1360, the illegitimate son of Dom Alvaro
Goncalves Pereira and Iria Goncalves do Carvalhal. The
sources for the life of Nuno are better than those for most
all of the order's medieval saints. There is a chronicle, author
unknown, dedicated to tracing his life, *Cronica do Condesta-
bre*, and he is frequently mentioned in Fernao Lopes's *Cron-
icas regias* since he was a major military and political figure
during the reign of King John I (reigned 1385–1433).

The first, anonymous chronicle is thought to have been written shortly after Nuno's death, sometime between 1431 and 1433. Lopes's chronicles were probably written between 1434 and 1450. Some historians warn that the anonymous chronicle was meant to portray Nuno in the most positive light, and consequently it should be treated gingerly by biographers (Monteiro 2017). In any case, given Nuno's prominence in the history of Portugal, there are many both legitimate historical works and hagiographic treatments of him.

Nuno's father, Dom Alvaro, was the prior of Crato, the head of the Order of St. John of Jerusalem in Portugal. As a professed Knight of Justice, Dom Alvaro was barred from marriage. However, this apparently did not prevent him from fathering at least thirty-two children (some accounts put the number much higher), one of whom was Nuno. Dom Alvaro himself was also illegitimate. His father, and therefore Nuno's grandfather, was Dom Goncalo Goncalves Pereira, the ninety-seventh archbishop of Braga. Both father, Dom Alvaro, and son, Nuno, were legitimized by royal decrees soon after their births.

Nuno's father was considered a great success as a knight of St. John. His exploits on the sea against the Turks brought him significant notice within the order, and in 1335, he was appointed prior of Crato, making him in effect the head of the Hospitallers in Portugal. He was a hero of the Battle of Salado (1340), which ended the threat of Muslim invasion of the Iberian Peninsula and secured control of the Straits of Gibraltar for the Christians. He was also a close advisor to three kings, Alfonso IV, Peter I, and Ferdinand I. The Portuguese Order of St. John flourished under his leadership, adding considerable property to its portfolio and expanding its prestige. Dom Alvaro's father, Archbishop Goncalo Pereira, preceded him as the head of the order in Portugal, and his son and Nuno's half-brother, Dom Peter Alvarez Pereira, succeeded Dom Alvaro probably around 1380. The connection between the Pereira family and the Hospitallers in Portugal was both close and enduring.

Through his paternal lineage, Nuno descended from the oldest Portuguese and Galician nobility, and he was a cousin to the founder of the noble Braganza family, the extant royal house of Portugal. His family had a long history of distinguished religious and military service. Since his father was the prior of Crato, Nuno grew up in the company of the knights of St. John of Jerusalem. It is likely, the chronicles say, that he was captivated by the chivalrous stories of Hospitallers defending the poor and weak and by the edifying tales of soldier-saints, like St. George, St. Martin, and St. James.

There is no reason to think that Nuno's education was any different from that of other young Portuguese aristocrats. In around 1373 at the age of thirteen, he found himself in the court of King Ferdinand I, known also as Ferdinand the Handsome (reigned 1367–1383), as page to Queen Leonor, a typical milestone for noble youth. He married three years later at the age of sixteen. The marriage produced one surviving daughter, Beatrice. At this point, Nuno decided to embark on a military career. He spent his first years fighting in skirmishes against Castile along the frontier, but his strategic mind and leadership skills were quickly evident to his superiors. By 1383, he was a widely respected young knight, ready to do his part when the country erupted in civil war.

The 1383–1385 crisis was precipitated by the death of King Ferdinand, who left no male heir to the throne. In April 1383, the Cortes (Assembly) met and chose John of Aviz, illegitimate son of King Peter I (reigned 1357–1367) and half-brother of Ferdinand, to fill the vacant throne. Challenged by the king of Castile, also named John, John of Aviz took up arms to defend his claim. By this time, Nuno had proven himself an outstanding military man, and he took command of John of Aviz's forces. The Pereira family was bitterly divided over this struggle for the throne, with Nuno and others supporting John of Aviz and Pedro fighting for the cause of Castile, whose claim was made by its Queen, the daughter of Portugal's late King Ferdinand.

Nuno proved himself an extraordinary military leader when in 1384 he led John of Aviz's armies to victory over the Castilians in the battle of Atoleiros. But the pivotal battle of the war was at Aljubarrota in 1385. Leading the Castilian forces was King John and his most effective general, Pedro Alvarez Pereira, half-brother to Nuno. Although outnumbered four to one, Nuno led John of Aviz's forces to victory and cleared the way for his coronation as King John I later that same year. With this victory, the Portuguese fully established their independence from Castile, and Nuno was given the supreme command of the kingdom's army with the title of constable and made the king's lord high steward. He apparently held both titles until his death in 1431, even if towards the end of his life, the titles were mostly honorific.

A desultory war continued on and off until a formal peace between Portugal and Castile was signed in 1411.

In the wake of the victory over Castile, Nuno was celebrated as a military genius, a founder of the modern Portuguese state, and a close confidant of the king. In short, the constable had a life of glory and honor awaiting him. The king showered him with titles and estates, and he became the most wealthy and powerful figure in the realm, except for King John himself. Gradually, however, it appears that any desire for praise, power, and wealth that he may have had weakened and ultimately disappeared. Over time, he used his great wealth to build multiple churches throughout Portugal dedicated to Our Lady, including the Carmelite church and monastery in Lisbon and the Church of Our Lady of Victories at Batalha.

In 1387, when Nuno was only in his late twenties, his wife died. It is said that instead of taking another wife, he vowed himself to celibacy for the rest of his life. Always a devout man even when commanding troops in the field, Nuno apparently grew in piety as he aged and his storied life continued. He prayed with his soldiers, encouraged them to attend Mass, and claimed his extraordinary victories on the battlefield were due to the intercession of the Blessed Virgin Mary. His piety, contemporaries say, included an intense devotion to Mary, admiration for the saintly knights St. James and St. George, and humility uncharacteristic for a nobleman of his standing.

According to many biographies, when peace between Portugal and Castile finally came, Nuno celebrated it by giving away the bulk of his wealth to the veterans of the war. In

1423, at the age of about sixty-three, an advanced age for the time, Nuno disposed of the rest of his wealth and, to the surprise of many, entered the Carmelite monastery in Lisbon as a lay brother, taking the name Brother Nuno of St. Mary. Some hagiographers point out Brother Nuno's action mirrored the recommendation in the Carmelite Rule of St. Albert: "Give up the armor of war and take on the spiritual armor of Carmel." There is, however, a background story to Nuno's divestment of his wealth.

No one can fairly dispute that there were high-minded motives behind Nuno's divesting himself of most of his material goods over a period of thirty years. However, historians remind us that there were practical motivations as well (Monteiro 2017). In 1393, Nuno began to give his veterans almost all the considerable number of estates that King John had granted to him for his extraordinary military exploits. The king was apparently not pleased when Nuno made these land grants to his men. It was not so much the fact they had been royal gifts. Rather, it was that in making these gifts, Nuno created a network of powerful vassals loyal to him. In effect, these estate grants provided Nuno with a standing army of men ready to fulfill their obligations to their liege lord. In all Portugal, only the king could raise a larger force by calling upon his vassals. Although John and Nuno apparently never broke their close friendship, it is understandable that the king would have been concerned by Nuno's actions (Monteiro 2017).

Around 1400, Nuno had to provide a large dowry for his daughter, Beatrice, upon her marriage to King John's younger son, Alfonso, the first Duke of Braganza. This was a second drain on his estate, although it likely remained the largest fortune in the realm. In 1423, the constable gave away the bulk of his remaining fortune prior to joining the Carmelites in Lisbon. Historians point out that Nuno parted with his wealth in a somewhat unusual way for the times. Instead of leaving it to his daughter through her husband, Alfonso, he left it directly to his three grandchildren. The normal manner of passing an estate was governed by primogeniture, or the passing of the inheritance intact to the eldest living male, who would have been the Duke of Braganza, his daughter's husband. However, this would have been highly disadvantageous to two of his three grandchildren. So Nuno left each of them a share of his estate, with the rest going to the Carmelite convent, his new home (Monteiro 2017).

The life of Nuno in the convent has, like those of many saints, been subjected to exaggeration and embellishment. One medievalist complained that through the years, the treatment of Nuno's religious life has been characterized by hagiographic "works that are aimed at the general public without the slightest concern about the critical examination of the sources" (Monteiro 2017). Some of the more popular hagiographies, which have served as unverifiable "sources" for much that is written about Nuno, were written by clerics (Salvini 1871; Santana 1745). Listed in Father Jose Pereira Santana's *Chronicle of the Carmelites* is apparently a roster of the many miracles associated with Nuno, most of which involved curing of children from various maladies and saving ships and seaman from nautical disasters.

It is said that Brother Nuno's preference would have been to withdraw to a community far away from Lisbon, but the son of the king, Don Duarte (Edward), prevented it. Edward apparently felt that the holy constable was a national figure who could not entirely wall himself off from the people. In the monastery, Brother Nuno wanted no special treatment because of his status or because he had built the monastery and continued to fund it. However, it is probably safe to say that the other Carmelites were in awe of having such a well-known national figure and their own benefactor as a serving brother and treated him accordingly.

Nevertheless, Nuno chose the humblest rank of lay brother, signaling that he wanted to end out his years in quiet prayer and service. He apparently willingly undertook the lowliest of duties, and he continued his service to the poor, organizing the daily distribution of food. He was known inside and outside the convent for his prayer, his devotion to the Mother of God, and his practice of penance: a man who turned his back on power, wealth, and prestige to live contentedly as a simple serving brother.

On his deathbed in 1431 Brother Nuno was visited by King John, who considered him to be his best friend. It was, after all, Nuno who helped to establish John's rule in Portugal by defeating the Castilian armies on the field and defending for thirty-nine years Portugal's borders before entering the monastery.

Dom Nuno Alvares Pereira, constable of Portugal and Carmelite brother, died on Easter Sunday, April 1, 1431. His funeral was a most solemn celebration, with the participation of the entire royal court. He was buried in the Carmelite church of Lisbon. Upon his death, Nuno was immediately acclaimed a saint by the people, who called him

"Holy Constable." His cult continued to grow, fueled by the many documented miracles at his tomb. King Edward, John I's son, had a silver lamp, which burned continuously, placed on Nuno's tomb.

From time to time in Portuguese history, the person of the holy constable was politicized, used to justify or attack various political positions. Perhaps this is the reason that his formal canonization took so long, even though he was considered by the people a holy man from the moment of his death, if not before. For instance, in the late nineteenth and early twentieth centuries, Nuno was held up as a role model and publicly admired by rightwing politicians and monarchists. They portrayed him as a paragon of Portuguese values, a restorer of Portuguese greatness, a fighter against internal decay, and a savior from the republican left (Leal 2000; Gori 2010). The fact that he was co-opted by various Portuguese political factions likely did not facilitate his path to sainthood.

Further, St. Nuno's connections to the Order of St. John (Malta) may at first seem somewhat tenuous, as they appear to be based on familial ties alone. Of course, the fact that Nuno's father, Don Alvaro, was an accomplished and celebrated prior of Crato and head of the Hospitallers in Portugal for about forty years, as was his grandfather, Archbishop Goncalo Pereira, is not the only reason. St. Nuno's life very much reflected the Hospitaller values that he had learned as a child and young man: *Tuitio Fidei et Obsequium Pauperum* (protection of faith and service to the poor). He combined a military career with a devout Christian life and care for the poor and weak, much like the Knights of St. John.

It is interesting to note that the cause for St. Nuno went through the modern process for canonization, even though he was treated as a saint for hundreds of years prior to his beatification in the early twentieth century and canonization in the twenty-first century. The Vatican apparently did not accept the *Chronicle of the Carmelites*' list of miracles as sufficient or credible enough to qualify for sainthood. It took a second modern miracle, attributed to Nuno in 2000, to ensure the success of his cause.

In 1918, Brother Nuno was beatified by Pope Benedict XV and canonized ninety-one years later on April 26, 2009 by Pope Benedict XVI. The Order of Malta and the Carmelite Order celebrate his feast day on November 6.

Collect From the Missal of the Sovereign Military Order of Malta

O God, who called Saint Nuno to lay down the weapons of this world and follow Christ under the protection of the Blessed Virgin, grant through the intercession of this former member of our Order that we too may deny ourselves and cling to you with all our hearts. Through the same Jesus Christ your Son, who lives and reigns with you and the Holy Spirit, one God, for ever and ever.

Early Modern Saints

The Fifteenth through the Eighteenth Centuries

11

The English Martyrs

Blessed Adrian Fortescue, Blessed Frá David Gonson, and Venerable Frá Thomas Dingley

The social and political turmoil unleashed by King Henry VIII's (1491–1547) decision to break with Rome and establish an English national church with the king as its head fatally engulfed three knights of the Order of Malta: Sir Adrian Fortescue, Frá David Gonson (Gunston), and Frá Thomas Dingley. All three were executed (Fortescue and Dingley in 1539 and Gonson in 1541) for refusing to abjure the pope and recognize Henry as the supreme authority of the Church in England.

The England of these three knights of St. John was dominated by the willful and capricious Tudor king Henry VIII, who ascended the throne in 1509 and ruled until his death in 1547 at the age of fifty-five. Under his father, Henry VII (1457–1509), the first Tudor king and the last English king to win his throne in battle (War of the Roses, Battle of Bosworth Fields, 1485), England pursued a policy of détente with Spain. King Henry VII arranged for the marriage of his eldest son and heir, Prince Arthur, to Catherine of Aragon, the youngest daughter of the famed Spanish rulers, King

Ferdinand and Queen Isabella. The wedding took place in November 1501.

Less than five months after the marriage ceremony, Prince Arthur died unexpectedly at the age of fifteen. To preserve the alliance with Spain, King Henry decided to betroth his younger son and now his heir, ten-year-old Henry, to Catherine. This prospect was welcomed in the Spanish court, and in 1503 Catherine, the widow of Prince Arthur, was betrothed to the new heir to the English throne, Prince Henry. When Henry came of age, he rejected the engagement, but shortly after Henry VII died in 1509, the young prince agreed to marry Catherine, as his father had wished. He and his new queen were enthroned with great pomp and ceremony on June 23, 1509.

Adrian Fortescue was born around 1476. He was in his early thirties when Henry VIII ascended the throne. The Fortescue family traced its roots to Richard La Fort, who served in the retinue of William the Conqueror at the Battle of Hastings in 1066. The victory at Hastings sealed the Norman conquest of England. La Fort was said to have saved William's life when the Conqueror's horse was slain from under him by covering his lord with his shield. Thus, the family motto: *Forte scutum salus ducum* (A strong shield [for] the safety of leaders).

The Fortescues were faithful supporters of the Tudors and Lancastrians in the War of the Roses. Under Henry VI, who reigned from 1422 to 1461 and again from 1470 to 1472, Sir John Fortescue was lord chief justice of England and, later around 1442, lord chancellor. His son, also John, continued the family's strong support for the Tudors, holding several important offices under Henry VII. In turn, his son, Adrian, served under both Henry VII and Henry VIII.

In 1513, Sir Adrian was called upon by Henry VIII to raise a contingent of men and arms to accompany the king to France, attacking that country in support of England's continental allies. The incursion was brief but successful, and Sir Adrian returned to England with the king in October 1513, four months after disembarking in Calais.

Again in 1522, Sir Adrian was called upon by the king to join, with a specified number of armed men, in a campaign against the French. Henry was in alliance with the Holy Roman Empire whose ruler, Charles V, had declared war on France. Sir Adrian served under the Earl of Surrey from May to October in a successful raid on French territory that brought much plundered wealth, if not territorial gain.

In August 1523, the Duke of Suffolk crossed over to Calais with, according to contemporary chronicles, Sir Adrian among the duke's retinue. This sizeable English force captured several French towns but suffered through a bitterly cold winter, returning to Calais in a weakened state. The Crown called on Sir Adrian once again in 1528, but instead of demanding the presence of Sir Adrian, Henry simply specified the number of men and arms that he expected his vassal to furnish. At some point probably around the time of the French campaigns, Henry appointed Sir Adrian as a gentleman to the king's privy chamber, a notable public mark of royal favor.

In 1527, Henry VIII began his effort to annul his eighteen-year marriage to Queen Catherine, thus disrupting the peace of the realm for the rest of his reign and well beyond. Catherine had failed to produce a male heir, having had four stillborn babies, one male child who died at seven weeks old, and Mary, who was born in 1516. Arguing that his union with Catherine should be annulled because he married his brother's wife, Henry appealed to Pope Clement VII for a divorce. When in 1529 it became clear that the pope was not willing to annul the marriage, Henry turned on his lord chancellor, Cardinal Thomas Wolsey, whom the king blamed for failing to successfully persuade the pope. In 1530, Wolsey was accused of high treason. He died of natural causes while traveling to London to answer the charge.

In 1533, the new archbishop of Canterbury, Thomas Cranmer, a secret reform sympathizer, defied the pope and dissolved the marriage of Henry and Catherine. The king wasted little time in marrying his mistress, Anne Boleyn, a first cousin of Sir Adrian Fortescue. Anne gave birth to a girl, the future Queen Elizabeth I, shortly thereafter. Sir Adrian seems to have remained in the good graces of the Crown, even after the start of trouble between Henry and the pope in 1527. In 1530, it appears that he was even granted some land expropriated from the estate of the dead and disgraced Cardinal Wolsey, and he maintained a good relationship with his cousin, Queen Anne. Apparently, Sir Adrian kept his views to himself on the "King's Great Matter": Henry's annulment, his subsequent marriage, and the issue of the supremacy of the English church.

In 1532, at the age of fifty-six, Sir Adrian was admitted into the Order of St. John of Jerusalem. Widowed and remarried, he had a total of seven children. It was curious timing to enter the Order of Malta, just as the storm clouds were gathering and sides were being taken in the struggle between pope and king. Instead of avoiding controversy, Sir Adrian appeared to be stalking it. In 1534, just two years after Sir Adrian entered the order, the Act of Succession was promulgated by Parliament, excluding Mary, the daughter of Catherine, from the line of succession in favor of her half sister, Elizabeth.

Sir Adrian must have been struck by the refusal of two prominent figures, Bishop John Fisher and former lord chancellor Thomas More, to take the oath of succession. Subsequently, both men also refused to take the oath to the 1534 Act of Supremacy that declared the "king was the only supreme head of the Church of England on earth." They were accused of high treason and both beheaded in 1535. With mounting trepidation, faithful Catholic aristocrats may well have wondered that if such luminaries of the realm could be treated in such a manner, what was in store for them?

On August 29, 1534 while on a business trip, Sir Adrian was detained in the town of Shirburn and transported to Marshalsea, a prison considered to be a tolerable place of confinement. It seems as if he was held there at least until February 1535, but it is not known whether he was sent home under house arrest or held temporarily elsewhere in London. Nor is it known the exact reason for his detention. In the meantime, events pressed on relentlessly. Thomas More and Bishop Fisher were executed on the same day in July 1535. Queen Catherine died of natural causes in January 1536. Anne Boleyn, Sir Adrian's cousin, was beheaded in May of the same year, the day after which Henry married Jane Seymour.

At some point in late 1584 or early 1585, it is believed that Sir Adrian was released and permitted to return home, but his entire household was under suspicion. It was only a matter of time until the authorities came for him. The uncovering of the Exeter Conspiracy involving the Marques of Exeter, the Countess of Salisbury, and the aristocratic Pole family and others may have been the perfect excuse to gather in Sir Adrian. The conspirators were arrested in November 1538 and taken to the Tower. In February 1539, almost two years after the beheading of his cousin, Anne Boleyn, Sir Adrian was arrested and taken to the Tower.

Cromwell had earlier petitioned the courts for an unprecedented interpretation of the law that would allow a conviction and execution without a hearing of evidence. The petition was granted, and now it was to be used against the accused participants in the Exeter Conspiracy. Sir Edward Neville was executed within weeks of his arrival at the Tower. In January 1539, the Marques of Exeter and Baron Montagu were found guilty of treason and executed. Sir Geoffrey Pole was acquitted and released. The family's extensive wealth and property was confiscated by the Crown. Not one of the accused had recourse even to a sham trial or a simple presentation of the evidence. When Sir Adrian arrived at the Tower in February 1539, he joined the remaining Exeter conspirators, as well as a fellow knight of St. John, Frá Thomas Dingley.

Not a great deal is known about Sir Thomas Dingley. He was born about 1507 into the country gentry of Boston in Lincolnshire to a family with a history in the Order of St. John. His maternal uncle, Sir William Weston, was the order's powerful lord prior of England from 1527 to 1540. Sir Thomas entered the order in May 1526 and eventually became a professed Knight of Justice. Throughout his tenure in the order, Frá Thomas was the beneficiary of the support and patronage of his uncle, the lord prior. Eventually, young Frá Thomas was made preceptor of Baddesley and preceptor of Mayne. He was also a regular traveler to Malta, where he was known as Tomasso Dingli. There he accumulated lands and endowed several churches.

Frá Thomas was very well connected both within the order and in English aristocratic circles. In 1536, just a year before Dingley was sent to the Tower, King Henry himself wrote a letter to the grand master in Malta asking him to bestow on Frá Thomas "the next preceptor which shall fall vacant." This letter is just one of several that outline the controversy involved in the competition to become the preceptor of Schingay, a lucrative estate in Cambridgeshire owned by the order. Several Knights of Justice believed that Frá Thomas was undeserved of yet another sinecure and that he was unfairly using his connections to further his aims.

In January 1537, Frá Ambrose Cave, who was lobbying to secure Schingay for himself, wrote to Thomas Cromwell. In the letter, Frá Ambrose expressed confidence that Cromwell will be on his side in "the controversy between [me] and Mr. Dyngley [sic] for the commandry of Shingay [sic]." Further, he goes on to criticize the presumptuousness and entitlement of such a young knight who does not seem to respect the traditions of the order. (Dingley was about thirty years old when Frá Ambrose penned this letter.)

"If Dyngley has it [Schingay], no man will be preferred but himself, for he would then keep two commandries, besides . . . the priory worth 40L a year, and a pension out of another commandry of 100 cr. . . . No man for so little time serving the Religion [Order of St. John] is so rewarded. He should be content and not seek means to break the ancient style and custom of the Religion" (Cave to Cromwell, January 13, 1537).

Despite the opposition of several professed knights, Frá Thomas took possession of Schingay on April 19, 1537 when King Henry confirmed the decision of the grand master, "not withstanding that the said office is in litigation between Ambrose Cave and the said Thomas."

In this case, however, the king's word was not to be the last. Frá Ambrose continued to seek a way to overturn the award of Schingay to Frá Thomas. Just six months later, Frá William Weston, Thomas's uncle and the lord prior of England, warned his nephew that Cave had succeeded in persuading Cromwell to overturn the decision. It is at this point that Dingley appears to have been denounced for his conduct at the residence of the English ambassador to Genoa.

Dingley was alleged to have said that the king was bloodthirsty and to have spoken in favor of Henry's overthrow. After Dingley's execution, the British ambassador to Malta, Sir Clement West, in a letter to Cromwell, says that the "osspeteler" [Hospitaller] told him that Dingley had denounced King Henry for executing people arbitrarily "for any old reason."[1] Clearly, some within the order were speaking against Frá Thomas. Frá Ambrose Cave, Dingley's rival for Schingay, had mounted a furious campaign to undermine Frá Thomas's reputation with Cromwell. It is possible that Cave may have shared with Cromwell or others some of Frá Thomas's more indiscreet comments about the king. Dingley was also involved as a key witness in the sensational arrest of another Catholic notable, Sir George Throckmorton, a member of Parliament who was ultimately cleared and released. Frá Thomas's role as a witness to Sir George's criticisms of the king may well have further fueled the authorities' suspicions of Dingley.

On September 18, 1537, Sir Thomas was charged with high treason and committed to the Tower. He apparently remained in prison for almost eighteen months before his fellow knight of St. John, Sir Adrian Fortescue, joined him in the Tower. There can be little doubt that the two were known to each other, but there is no documentation of a relationship either before or after imprisonment. The Crown insisted that both were guilty of high treason for plotting against the king, albeit in separate conspiracies. Sir Adrian was suspected of involvement in the Exeter Conspiracy, while Frá Thomas was linked to foreign intrigues while abroad in Malta and elsewhere and was, according to

---

[1]   Some historians (Peter Marshall and Geoffrey Scott, eds. *Catholic Gentry in English Society*. New York: Routledge, 2016) believe that Thomas Dingley was betrayed by his fellow knights of St. John who bitterly resented his accumulation of wealth and influence so quickly and, they felt, undeservedly. There is no definitive evidence that this was the case, although there does seem reason enough to further investigate.

witnesses, condemned by his own words uttered against the king. Neither one was permitted a trial.

Sir Adrian's offences were more directly linked to his refusal to publicly take the succession and supremacy oaths than to his supposed involvement in the Exeter Conspiracy. He apparently followed, to the same end, the path of Thomas More, thinking that if he never voiced an opinion on the King's Great Matter, he would be safe. Such was not the case for either Sir Adrian Fortescue or Sir Thomas More. Frá Thomas Dingley appears to have been far less discreet in sharing his opinions and perhaps too trustful of his fellow knights.

Neither man, however, betrayed his faith. Whether or not they were involved in various treasonous plots, which is doubtful, their real offence was not recognizing publicly the supremacy of Henry over the pope. Cromwell often offered Tower prisoners, as he did to Thomas More and John Fisher, their lives if they would publicly attend an Anglican service or take the oath of supremacy. It took heroic courage and unshakeable faith to remain constant to the Church and the Order of Malta in sixteenth-century England. Sir Adrian Fortescue and Sir Thomas Dingley, despite whatever failings their earthly lives may have exhibited, refused in the end to compromise their beliefs though they forfeited their lives. On July 8, 1539, they were taken from the Tower and beheaded.

Sometime in mid-1540, after his brothers in religion gave their lives for the Faith, Sir David Gonson (Gunston), a professed knight and the Order of St. John's third English martyr, returned to England from Malta. He had apparently been abroad, largely at the convent in Malta for several years. He was admitted to the order in 1533 at the English auberge in Malta and continued his military training and religious formation on the island.

Sir David came from a family well-known for its service to the Tudors. His father was given the rank of vice admiral of Norfolk and Suffolk and served as treasurer of the Navy. He was one the three "founders" of the modern Royal Navy and a close advisor to Henry VIII. Sir David's brother, Benjamin, also pursued a successful career in the Navy, serving on the Navy Board and holding royal appointments as both surveyor of the Navy and, like his father, treasurer of the Navy.

In Malta, Frá David was also pursuing a naval career, serving on the warships of the order's impressive navy in fulfillment of his three-year general service requirement. As a young man, Frá David seems to have had a somewhat boisterous nature. While in Malta, he had a bloody altercation for reasons unknown with two other English knights, Sir Philip Babington and Sir Christopher Myres. All three Knights of Justice were temporarily stripped of their religious habits and imprisoned for nine months on the island of Gozo. After prison, they were reinstated to their ranks, although later, Myres was accused of murder and banished from the order.

In 1540, having been fully restored to his rank in the order, Frá David returned to England to find the country still in great turmoil over the religious upheaval brought on by the Supremacy Act. His brethren, Sir Adrian Fortescue and Frá Thomas Dingley, had just recently been beheaded.

In 1536, the monasteries and convents were closed and their wealth confiscated, sparing at first the order's property since the king did not view its houses as proper monasteries. The 1534 Succession Act, with its supremacy preamble, generated continued opposition among Catholic aristocrats.

In 1539, the year before Gonson's return to England, the king had finally turned his full attention to the Knights of St. John. He declared himself the de facto head of the Order of St. John in England, insisting that all new members be approved by the Crown and take the oath to the king. Further, those knights appointed to commanderies could not recognize or promote the "jurisdiction, authority, rank, or title of the bishop of Rome." As expected, the grand master rejected these conditions, knowing full well where this repudiation would lead.

In May 1540, Parliament enacted a law suppressing the Order of St. John and authorizing the confiscation of its considerable wealth and properties throughout the kingdom. In October, the Privy Council, on the word of Sir Philip Babington and the complaint of John Story, charged Frá David with high treason. Apparently, Babington had not forgotten his altercation with Gonson in Malta. Frá David, while abroad, was accused of publicly and repeatedly denying the supremacy of the king in spiritual and religious matters, branding the king, and all who aided him, "heretics," and rejecting the validity of the law that denied Henry's subjects the right to appeal to the pope.

Despite the delicacy of charging the son of Vice Admiral Gonson with treason, the Privy Council had Frá David arrested and brought to the Tower in October 1540. On

July 12, 1541, after months of torture, Frá David Gonson was dragged through the streets to St. Thomas Waterings, hanged until almost dead, his entrails drawn from his body while still alive, and his body broken into quarters by four horses. His conviction for high treason, like Fortescue's and Dingley's, came without a trial or presentation of evidence. His alleged disloyalty to the Crown does not appear to have harmed his father's or brother's standing with the king. They both continued in the service of Henry—although perhaps in what was a telling tragedy, the vice admiral killed himself in 1544.

Sir Adrian Fortescue, Frá Thomas Dingley, and Frá David Gonson, the English martyrs, have a special place in the heroic history of the Order of Malta. For among the order's twenty venerated men and women, these sixteenth-century Englishmen comprise most of the order's recognized martyrs. Their lives, like the lives of all saints, were not perfect or without failings. They were not authors of beautiful prayers, nor were they known for their intense spirituality. They did not pass through life working miracles and wonders. They were, however, men of the religion made for their times: courageous in the face of extreme physical torture, faithful and constant though it cost them their lives, and holy examples to their beleaguered countrymen faced with life and death dilemmas.

Blessed Adrian Fortescue was beatified in by Pope Leo XIII in 1895. Blessed David Gonson was beatified by Pope Pius XI in 1929. Venerable Thomas Dingley was declared worthy of veneration by Pope Leo XIII in 1886. Blessed

Adrian Fortescue's feast day is celebrated on July 8, Blessed David Gonson's on July 12.

Collects From the Missal of the Sovereign Military Order of Malta

O God, who made Blessed David an outstanding champion of the Catholic faith, grant, we pray, that he who shed luster on our Order by his martyrdom may inspire us to defend the unity of the Church. Through our Lord Jesus Christ, your Son, who lives and reigns with you in the unity of the Holy Spirit, one God, forever and ever.

Grant, we pray, almighty God, that we who honor the heavenly birthday of the Martyr Blessed Adrian may, by his intercession, be strengthened in the love of our name and faithfully hold fast to your holy Church until death. Through our Lord Jesus Christ, your Son, who lives and reigns with you in the unity of the Holy Spirit, one God, forever and ever.

Saints of the Modern Era

The Nineteenth through the Twenty-First Centuries

12

Blessed Charles of Austria

1887–1922

Charles (Karl) was born into the Habsburg imperial family on August 17, 1887 to Archduke Otto, a nephew of Emperor Franz-Josef (1848–1916), and the archduke's wife, Maria Josefa of Saxony. Charles was the last emperor of the Austro-Hungarian Dual Monarchy. He died on April 1, 1922 in exile in Portugal.

When Charles was born in 1887, he was considered a rather distant heir to the throne. Emperor Franz Joseph, who ruled from 1848 to 1916, had a son and heir, Archduke Rudolf, destined to mount the thrones of the dual monarchy. However, Rudolf took his own life in 1889, two years after Charles was born, although the palace tried its best to pass the suicide off as a hunting accident. Because the emperor had only the one son, his nephew, Archduke Franz Ferdinand, became the heir. Franz Ferdinand, however, had made a morganatic marriage. His children were thus disqualified from the line, making Charles's father, Otto, the next in line to the throne behind his elder brother Franz Ferdinand.

In 1906, at the age of nineteen, Charles unexpectedly took his father's place in the line of succession when Otto died prematurely after contracting a disease on a trip to the Holy Land. Although it was clear then that the young Archduke Charles was certain to ascend the throne, his coronation, it was thought, would not be until his uncle, Franz Ferdinand, died, presumably decades into the twentieth century.

Charles's biographers generally agree about his personality and character. Even as a boy, he apparently showed signs of a strongly empathetic nature, demonstrating an interest in the plight of the unfortunate. His mother, Archduchess Maria Josefa, who was renowned throughout the empire for her charitable works and concern for the poor, encouraged young Charles in this direction. As a child, he sold fruits and vegetables from his garden in the Persenbeu castle and gave the money to the poor. He would also go through his wardrobe and quietly distribute his clothes to those in need.

By all accounts, Charles was an honest, fair-minded, serious youngster, and aware of the fact that he would one day sit on the four-hundred-year-old Habsburg throne, he was diligent about preparing himself properly. He was devout and religious, attending daily Mass as far as possible throughout his life, even as a war-time emperor. Charles was fortunate to marry a princess of royal blood whom he genuinely loved, Zita of Bourbon Palma, the daughter of the last independent ruler of Parma, Duke Robert (reigned 1854–1859). Zita shared Charles's piety and devotion to the Church. She was an active support for her husband both before and after his accession to the throne, and her diaries provide a valuable insight into Charles's brief life. Married in 1911, their union produced eight children, five boys and three girls. On their wedding day, the young archduke was purported to have said to his bride, "Now, you and I must help each other to get to heaven."

The assassination of the heir apparent, Archduke Franz Ferdinand, and his wife, Sofie, in Sarajevo in 1914 sparked the outbreak of the First World War (1914–1918) and dramatically changed Charles's and Zita's lives. Suddenly, as Zita recounts in her diary, Charles was heir to the throne, a development that the royal couple did not expect for decades, and he was next-in-line to the eighty-four-year-old Emperor Franz Josef. At any moment, during the brewing conflict, young Archduke Charles might be called upon to assume the throne, a throne that sat upon the wobbly foundations of what some contemporaries considered an unviable multinational society.

The Dual Monarchy of Austria and Hungary was much more ethnically diverse than its moniker implies. The monarchy was dominated politically by the Austrians and the Hungarians, who were considered equal partners joined by the ruler of the House of Habsburg-Lorraine. The emperor ruled in Hungary as king and was separately crowned in Budapest upon ascending to the throne. This "dual" structure of the empire was the result of a compromise in 1868 between the dominant nationalities, the Germans and Hungarians. Political power, such as it was under the emperors, was closely held by these two ethnic groups, although there were a total of eighteen recognized nationalities and languages. The polyglot army's official language was German, and the military swore allegiance not to the state but to the person of the emperor-king.

By the outbreak of war in 1914, Franz-Josef had ruled this collection of nationalities living across a wide swath of central, southeastern, and eastern Europe for sixty-six years. When he died on November 28, 1916, he left his great nephew, Charles, a country engaged in a crippling war and struggling to maintain the loyalty of the various ethnic groups, particularly the Czechs and South Slavs who had been agitating for decades for greater autonomy under the dual monarchy. The new emperor, Charles I in the Austrian lands and Charles IV as king of Hungary, was twenty-nine years old.

The brief two-year reign of Charles was marked by his unceasing efforts to secure an honorable peace and to end the horrors of the war. Upon assuming the throne, his proclamation read: "I will do everything to banish in the shortest possible time the horrors and sacrifices of war, to win back for my peoples the sorely missed blessings of peace."

The emperor was not a pacifist; he had served in combat positions of leadership in the army during the first years of the war, although every possible effort was made to ensure his safety as heir apparent. Still, he was a firsthand witness of the terrible carnage of the First World War, and his strong inclination was to end the horrific bloodshed of modern trench warfare. Charles's desire for peace was also practical, for he was convinced that if the empire continued the war much beyond 1916, it might very well split apart into quarreling ethnic centers, threatening the very existence of the ancient Habsburg dynasty.

There is no historical debate about the intensity of Charles's desire for peace. Indeed, his persistent attempts to seek peace—separately, if necessary, from his German ally—almost collapsed the monarchy in what is known as the Sixtus Affair. Intent on bringing an end to hostilities, Charles reached out to the French and British through his brother-in-law, Prince Sixtus of Bourbon Parma, proposing secret peace negotiations. The talks failed to materialize, but the letters from the emperor were made public, incensing the Germans. Charles and Austria-Hungary weathered the ensuing storm, and he continued to attempt to bring an end to the war by approaching President Woodrow Wilson. These efforts also failed, but not because of Charles. The responsibility for the failure lies with Wilson's intransigence and his vacillating approach to negotiations.

Historians often underestimate, or even ignore, the third reason that Charles pursued peace with such tenacity, a tenacity that earned him the moniker "the Peace Emperor": his truly devout Christian nature and deeply imbedded Catholicism. Charles viewed his responsibilities and purpose in life as having come from God. He took very seriously his obligation to serve his people and reflected carefully on the moral ramifications of his actions. He saw firsthand the suffering that the war had engendered and viewed it as his Christian duty to release his people from what was fast becoming a chaotic hell.

Cardinal Christoph Schonborn, archbishop of Vienna in the late twentieth and early twenty-first centuries, said of Charles: "Can a politician possibly live a modest and holy life? These questions are constantly posed concerning the beatification of Karl of the House of Austria. Every person—wherever God has placed him—is destined for holiness. People in positions of responsibility, decision-makers, such as politicians and business leaders, as well as bishops, are challenged by special circumstances, but are by no means exempt from this call to holiness."

Some contemporaries described Charles as "good, kind and brave." Others cited his "strength of character," his holding fast to his beliefs, and his patience in pursuing his ideals. Still others saw him as a man of conviction, integrity, and conscience formed by his Catholic faith (Brook-Shephard 1968). He was invested in the Order of Malta as a Knight, Grand Cross of Honor and Devotion with Honorary Profession. Although he obviously was not active in the order, the emperor shared its concern for the poor and marginalized and its commitment to defend the Faith.

With the entry of the United States into the war in 1917, the scales were tipped in favor of the Allies. In late 1918 and early 1919, the Central Powers' ability to continue the war was weakening. Although Germany's and Austria-Hungary's armies seemed well positioned, their home fronts were collapsing into revolutionary chaos. The dual monarchy, as Charles and others had feared, began to split into competing nationalities and separate countries, led by the Czechs and the South Slavs.

The view of several key players in the fall of the empire was that Charles was a well-intentioned, decent moral young man, but he was entirely too weak to stop the downward spiral of the dual monarchy. Charles could not give effective support to the Hungarian politicians who supported his views on ending the war and extending suffrage in Hungary. Count Mihaly Karolyi was one such personality who at one point was led to believe that the king would appoint him prime minister of Hungary to work for peace and domestic reform. But Charles did not have the stomach to take on a fight with the reactionary prime minister, Count Istvan Tisza, an opponent of reforming the dual structure and a proponent of the German alliance.

Some historians, recognizing Charles's deep desire for peace and reform, nonetheless point out that he could have acted more decisively. He had the power by royal decree to reorganize the Austrian part of the empire on a federal basis, thus quelling the rising dissatisfactions among the ethnic minorities. In the Hungarian lands, they argue, Charles needed only to appoint a reform-minded government, perhaps with Karolyi at its head, to head off the growing instability of that state (Valiani 1973).

Once the last German offensive on the western front failed in late March 1918, all hope that Charles had for a separate peace was dashed. The allies now were only interested in unconditional surrender by Germany and its allies, without any guarantees of the future integrity of the Austro-Hungarian Empire. By April 1918, the British government was prepared to recognize the independence of the Austrian subject nationalities. London also made it clear that British forces would accept as friends and allies any subject nationalities on the front lines who defected to the Allies. From this point on, the dismemberment of the empire was almost a surety, and the fate of the royal family was sealed.

On March 24, 1919, the emperor and his family fled to Switzerland; however, Charles did not abdicate. Charles would make two failed attempts to regain the Hungarian throne in 1921. Both times, he was turned back by his former Admiral Nicholas Horthy, now serving as regent in place of the Habsburg king. The second attempt resulted in the exchange of gunfire, as Charles and his loyalists raced by train to Budapest and were met by Horthy's forces. Charles, however, refused to spill blood to regain his throne, ending his last attempt to restore the Habsburg house. In his memoirs, published after he was ousted by his erstwhile Nazi allies in 1945, Horthy said that he opposed the return of Charles in 1922 simply because the allies would have invaded Hungary rather than let a Habsburg sit again on the throne of St. Stephen. It was a weak and unconvincing argument, and the allegations of disloyalty to his monarch, to whom he had taken a personal oath, plagued Horthy for his entire life.

Eventually, Charles and his family settled on the Portuguese island of Madeira, forbidden by the Allies to return to the former Habsburg lands. He died in exile on April 1, 1922, his last words, according to Empress Zita, were, "I can't go on much longer. Thy will be done. Yes, yes, as you will it, Jesus." The last Habsburg emperor was thirty-five years old.

Charles was beatified by Pope St. John Paul II on October 3, 2004. The pope said that Charles saw his crown as representing a "holy service" to his people, and he sought to recognize and follow God's will in all things. In the end, although he lost his throne and died in exile, Emperor Charles lived a life of heroic virtue and stands, as Pope St.

John Paul II noted, as an example to all government leaders today. Blessed Charles I of Austria's feast day is celebrated on October 21.

Collect From the Missal of the Sovereign Military Order of Malta

O God, who through the trials of this life brought Blessed Karl from an earthly kingdom to a heavenly crown, grant to us, through his intercession, that by serving your Son and our neighbors we may attain eternal life. Through our Lord Jesus Christ, your Son, who lives and reigns with you in the unity of the Holy Spirit, one God, forever and ever.

Blessed Gerard, Founder. Public domain via Wikimedia Commons.

(*above*) St. Ubaldesca (oil on canvas), © Museum of the Order of St. John / Bridgeman Images.

(*left*) St. Nicasius (detail) from Madonna and Child between St. Francis and St. Nicasius (oil on poplar wood), by Giorgione. Public domain via Wikimedia Commons.

(*left*) Blessed Gerard of Villamagna (tempera on panel) by Bicci di Lorenzo. Public domain via Wikimedia Commons.

(*below*) Blessed Gerland of Germany, image from the Order of Malta in Rome (used with permission).

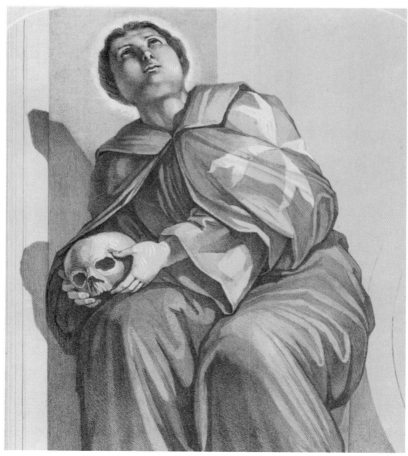

Blessed Peter Pattarini of Imola, image from the Order of Malta in Rome (used with permission).

(*left*) Santa Toscana of Verona (engraving), National Library of Malta, Valetta, photo © Leonard de Selva / Bridgeman Images.

(*below*) Adrian Fortescue (oil on canvas), © Museum of the Order of St. John / Bridgeman Images.

Blessed Charles of Austria. Photo from the George Grantham Bain collection at the Library of Congress, public domain via Wikimedia Commons.

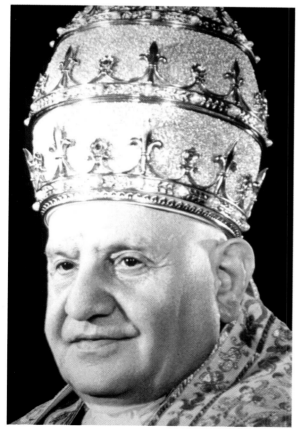

(*above left*) Blessed
Clemens August von
Galen, photo from the
picture collection of the
Münster Diocese archive, public domain via
Wikimedia Commons.

(*above right*) Blessed
Vilmos Apor c.1930,
photo public domain via
Wikimedia Commons.

(*left*) Pope St. John
XXIII, photo by Farabola / Bridgeman Images.

(*above*) Pope St. Paul VI, photo by Farabola / Bridgeman Images.

(*below*) Fra' Andrew Bertie, courtesy of SMOM archives. Used with permission.

13

Blessed Clemens August von Galen

1878–1946

Clemens August von Galen was born on March 16, 1878. He served as bishop of Munster, Germany from 1933 to his death in 1946. His persistent and outspoken criticism of the Nazi regime earned him the moniker the "Lion of Munster." He died in 1946, only weeks after being named a cardinal by Pope Pius XII.

Clemens August was the scion of an illustrious noble family closely attached to the Order of Malta. The family traced its roots in Germany's deeply Catholic Rhineland to the thirteenth century. He was born in the Castle Dinklage, his family's estate in lower Saxony, and grew up in a home life firmly rooted in the Catholic faith. His father, Count Ferdinand Heribert von Galen, was faithful to his noble and Catholic lineage, insisting on daily Mass for his thirteen children and leading the family in prayer each evening. His mother, Imperial Countess Elizabeth von Spee, was likewise devout. Both sides of the family routinely saw brothers, sisters, and cousins become priests and religious, and the von

Galens could point to relatives who had become bishops in the Munster diocese.

Clemens August, by all accounts a healthy child who eventually grew to over six and half feet tall, was imbued with this religious and clerical atmosphere. Deeply imbedded in this worldview were the recent memories of Otto von Bismark's (1815–1898) Kulturkampf, a bitter struggle between Catholics and the state over the role of the Church in German political and cultural life. From 1871 to 1878, this struggle was waged on many fronts, and Catholics, 36.5 percent of the newly unified German state, were depicted by Bismark and his allies as disloyal and obscurantist.

Concerned about the ramifications of the papal doctrine of infallibility for Germany, Bismark enacted laws that excluded clerics from education, banned the Jesuits and other religious orders, subordinated Church law to civil law, and required state approval for entrance into seminaries. The Church resisted these laws, with the pope attacking them as unjust and the German bishops calling for passive disobedience.

In Munster, the Kulturkampf was recalled with anger and bitterness. Its bishop, Johann Bernard Brinkmann, was imprisoned in 1875 and lived in exile in Holland from 1876 to 1884. Clemens August's father, Count Ferdinand Heribert, secretly visited the exiled bishop, despite government prohibitions against doing so. Bismark's persecution of the Church was not easily forgotten by German Catholics who were stung by accusations of disloyalty and treason and fearful of the resurgence of these attacks in later years (Griech-Polelle 2002).

Clemens August was educated by his mother and private tutors until he was twelve years old. In 1890, he and his younger brother, Franz, enrolled in Stella Matutina, the Jesuit boarding school in Feldkirch, Austria. After four years, young Clemens and his brother returned to Germany to complete their secondary school certifications. In 1897 Clemens August went to study philosophy in Fribourg, then on to the Jesuit University of Innsbruck. By this time, he had made up his mind to become a priest. He seriously considered the Jesuits, for whom he had great admiration, but the familial pull of Munster won out. He left Innsbruck and returned to Castle Dinklage. On May 28, 1904, Clemens August Count von Galen was ordained a priest of the Diocese of Munster. In 1916, he entered the Order of Malta as a Knight of Honor and Devotion.

Clemens August's first assignment was likely not very taxing: cathedral vicar and secretary to his own uncle, Bishop Max Gereon von Galen, auxiliary bishop of Munster. However, it gave the young priest a chance to tour the far-flung diocese and get to know its people and parishes. In 1906, Father von Galen was sent outside his diocese to Berlin to minister to the Catholic working class, and in 1919 he became pastor of St. Matthias Church in Berlin where he remained for ten years. Von Galen's twenty-three years in Berlin spanned difficult times for Germany: the defeat in World War I, the abdication of the kaiser, the post-war hyperinflation, the unstable Weimar Republic, and the rise of the Nazis and the radical right.

In 1929, von Galen was recalled to the Diocese of Munster and named pastor of St. Lambert's parish. Munster's Bishop

Poggenburg died on January 5, 1933, just weeks before Adolf Hitler was named chancellor of the German Reich. After several false starts involving candidates who removed their names from consideration, the cathedral chapter nominated Father von Galen as its candidate for bishop. The government approved the choice, and Pope Pius XI made the appointment of von Galen as bishop of Munster September 11, 1933.

Although von Galen was known for his patriotism, his appointment surprised some local Nazis in Munster who knew the outspoken and opinionated priest. Some wondered if the Nazis, in their zeal to make the first episcopal appointment under their regime as smooth as possible, had made a serious mistake in allowing von Galen to take the miter. In fact, Bishop von Galen is reported to have once said, "We von Galens may not be very good-looking or very smart, but we are Catholic to the bone." Eventually, the Nazis would understand just what von Galen meant (Utrecht 2016).

Although von Galen is famous for his powerful 1941 sermons attacking Nazi policies and ideologies, the bishop was a thorn in the side of Hitler's government from the outset of his episcopacy. Von Galen immediately crossed swords with Alfred Rosenberg, the Nazi ideologue who promoted the idea that Christianity was a myth that true Germans should reject. Rosenberg called for a return to the pagan gods of the pre-Christian German era. The bishop spoke out numerous times against Rosenberg's theories and even penned the introduction to a collection of anti-Rosenberg essays after Cardinal Schulte reneged on his commitment to support the book.

In 1936, the minister of interior and churches and schools, Julius Pauly, ordered that all crucifixes be removed from public places, including Catholic schools. In Oldenburg, part of the Munster diocese, the reaction was extreme: youth and women resigned en masse from Nazi organizations, a pastoral letter by von Galen condemning the action was read from every pulpit, and the people were in an uproar. Attempts to persuade and intimidate the protesters failed, and finally the government agreed to suspend the law in the diocese. The crosses stayed in the schools, but it was only a temporary victory. Despite von Galen's best efforts, Catholic and other denominational schools were virtually non-existent by 1939.

In 1937, Bishop von Galen was called to Rome by Pope Pius XI, along with four other German prelates, to discuss the preparation of the papal encyclical *Mitt Brennender Sorge* (With Burning Anxiety). Among the German bishops, von Galen stood out for his strong support of a full-throated, public criticism of Nazi violations of the 1933 concordat (treaty) between Germany and the Vatican. His views closely coincided with the pope's. The encyclical, a clearly worded, harsh attack on Nazi paganism, racial theories, and glorification of the state, was smuggled into Germany in March 1937. It was read at all the Palm Sunday Masses throughout Germany. Von Galen arranged for its clandestine printing and dissemination in his diocese, and he continued to promote its contents even as the government quietly, but brutally, dealt with the printers and disseminators of the encyclical.

From 1937 to 1939, Bishop von Galen fought a bitter, but losing, battle to preserve Catholic schools. After four years in power, the Nazis began to build "community" schools, launching an all-out effort to persuade parents to leave Catholic and other confessional schools in favor of the new schools. In Munster, the Church responded with a pastoral letter from its bishop directed to parents, urging them to remain steadfast in their support of Catholic schools. Soon, however, the Nazis turned the screws more tightly, preventing priests from entering Catholic schools to teach catechism. This rule even extended to von Galen, who was denied entry into the Catholic schools of Oldenburg.

Non-Catholic and even pagan teachers were hired, religious brothers and sisters were removed from the schools, and confessional schools were forcibly merged with the new community schools. "Religion" continued to be taught, but now by Nazi teachers untrained in Catholicism and more than willing to implement the Nazi curriculum. Von Galen was ceaseless in his opposition, telegramming Hitler himself, speaking out publicly, sending private notes of protest to government officials, and issuing several pastoral letters. It was all for naught. By the outbreak of the war with Poland, Catholicism had virtually been wiped out in German schools.

By 1940, Bishop von Galen was increasingly agitating among the German bishops for a more aggressive public stance against aspects of Nazism. This put him at odds with Cardinal Bertram, who had recommended to Pius XI in 1937 that the pope write a personal letter to Hitler instead of an encyclical to the German people. Von Galen was extremely outspoken, and he was clearly regarded by the Nazis as an enemy. When the Gestapo confiscated two Jesuit residences in Munster and expelled the Jesuits from Westphalia in July 1941, von Galen reacted furiously. Determined to attack the government's unjust expropriation of religious houses that had been happening throughout the Reich, he delivered the first of his three famous sermons at Sunday Mass on July 13, 1941, at a point in time when German armies were victorious in all of Europe.

The sermon of July 13 focused on the confiscation of the property of religious orders and the forcible ejection of the priests, brothers, and sisters from their homes, from the Munster diocese, and from Westphalia itself. Von Galen minced no words in his attack on the Gestapo, accusing it of imprisoning "innocent and well-respected" Germans without trials or hearings. He told his listeners that in the face of the power of the Gestapo, German citizens were "completely defenseless and unprotected." He reminded them that Germans had experienced this sort of unjust treatment at the hands of the Gestapo many times since the Nazis came to power. He told his listeners that they could not be sure that it would not someday happen to them. Innocent though they may be, he said, they will be "robbed of their freedom, thrown into cells and concentration camps." He accused the state of denying the people justice and, as if anticipating the government's reaction, said it was not his words that might weaken the war effort but the unjust actions of the Gestapo (Smith 1943).

The sermon had an electrifying impact. Copies were secretly produced and disseminated, reaching far beyond the border of the Munster diocese. Von Galen expected a visit from the

Gestapo and prepared himself to be arrested, but this did not happen. Apparently, Berlin remained fearful that should it touch the immensely popular bishop, all of Westphalia would be in a state of unrest. Unwilling to risk alienating the Catholic Rhineland, Hitler is purported to have said, "Bishop von Galen knows full well that after the war, I shall extract retribution to the last farthing" (Utrecht 2016).

On July 20, the bishop gave the second of his three celebrated sermons. He lamented that the confiscation of religious houses, which he had denounced the prior Sunday, continued unabated. He pointed out that many of the priests and brothers were away at the front, serving the Fatherland. While they were fighting for Germany, he said, the Gestapo was, without cause, expropriating their homes. He complained that no one in the government would listen to his appeals, claiming they had no authority over the Gestapo. Westphalia, said the bishop, had to struggle against two enemies, external and internal: the British who rained bombs on its cities and the Gestapo who persecuted the innocent and deprived them of justice and liberty.

In this second sermon, von Galen also touched upon the Nazi indoctrination of the youth, warning parents that their children were being taught to mistrust Christianity and hate the Church. Finally, he likened the struggle between Catholics and the state to an anvil and a hammer. The anvil, Catholics and the Church, is built to withstand the blows of the hammer, the state. He pointed out that the anvil always outlasts the hammer (Smith 1943).

This second sermon also created a stir among the people. The police noted that the Catholic population was agitated and disturbed by the bishop's words. Many questioned the actions of the Gestapo and wondered if Hitler knew that the religious houses were being confiscated and their inhabitants displaced. Again, the sermon was mimeographed and circulated clandestinely. Again, the Gestapo did not visit the bishop.

On August 3, 1941, von Galen gave the last of his three famous sermons. After some brief remarks criticizing the Gestapo, the bishop took up the issue of the killing of so-called "unproductive people." The German bishops had already in June 1941 issued a joint pastoral letter condemning the state-sponsored killing of the mentally ill. Von Galen took on the logical consequences of judging the worth of people's lives by the level of their productivity. If it were true, he said, that a life is measured by its value to the state, then not only will the mentally ill be killed but also the incurably sick, the disabled, the weak, and the aged.

Calling this "a horrible doctrine," von Galen warned that he had seen evidence that indicated that very soon a general round-up of the "unproductive" from hospitals and nursing homes would begin. Once this happens, the bishop said, it can extend to everyone who in old age become weak and infirm. Even German men who sacrificed limbs and mental well-being for the Fatherland may, upon their return home, find themselves liquidated as "unproductive." Such a program risked destroying morale on the front, von Galen warned. It only takes one secret order, he prophesized, to extend the murdering of the mentally ill to anyone deemed to be of no use to society. The outcry against the euthanasia program, led by von Galen, was so great that Hitler suspended the program, only to take it up more secretly in 1943.

This third sermon, in which von Galen also enumerated how the state was violating every one of the Ten Commandments, received wide circulation. According to Phillip Freiherr von Boeselager, one of the Valkyrie conspirators responsible for the failed 1944 attempt on Hitler's life, Bishop von Galen's sermons were widely discussed and appreciated among soldiers on the frontlines (Boeselager 2009). They inspired the young resisters of Munich's White Rose organization. They were even read on Allied radio and dropped as propaganda leaflets on German lines, developments that disturbed the patriotic prelate.

Von Galen survived the war and proved to be as difficult to the Allied occupying forces as he was to Hitler's regime. He hectored the British commander on a variety of issues: food and shelter for his people, rampant crime, and the Allied notion of "collective guilt" for the Nazi crimes. On February 18, 1946, Bishop von Galen was raised to cardinal by Pope Pius XII in Rome. It was the first time in its seven-hundred-year history that the Munster Diocese had a cardinal as its ordinary.

On March 16, 1946, Cardinal Clemens August von Galen was officially welcomed home to his diocese. It was his sixty-eighth birthday. Fifty thousand people jammed the flag and banner bedecked streets of the ruined city to greet von Galen. Weeks earlier, he had been raised to the rank of bailiff in the Order of Malta. On this day, he was escorted by a contingent of knights of Malta who, having been refused permission by the British to wear their uniforms with swords, were arrayed in black suits.

In remarks before his ruined cathedral, Cardinal von Galen thanked his people for their faith in the Church and their unswerving support that saved him from martyrdom. He told the crowd that he spoke out for thousands of Germans who believed that Germany must be based on Christianity but had no way to express this belief under the Nazi regime. He celebrated his first pontifical Mass the next day, took to his bed with stomach ailments on March 19, and died of complications from a ruptured appendix on March 22, 1946.

Blessed von Galen was not a complicated man. He was a man whose entire existence was measured by his faithfulness to Catholicism and to the Church. He saw the world as essentially black and white, and he took very seriously his role as teacher and protector of the people of his diocese. Although a man of faith who was passionately devoted to the Blessed Mother and the Eucharist, people did not remember him as overly pious or devout. They viewed him as a warrior for the Faith, as the "Lion of Munster." His noble bearing and his physical stature made him an imposing figure, but he was said to be gentle with children and to exude the warmth of a favorite grandfather.

Some historians criticize von Galen because he did not speak out specifically on behalf of unbaptized Jews. Others, the majority, recognize the difficulties inherent in publicly advocating for the Jews inside the Nazi state and point out that von Galen truly believed that by speaking out directly, he would only make things worse for Jews and Catholics alike (Griech-Polelle 2002). Nevertheless, the very first battle he fought with the Nazis in 1933 was over his stubborn opposition to the injection of anti-Semitism into the educational curriculum. His pastoral letters and sermons frequently mentioned the rights of people regardless of race. He repeatedly criticized the treatment of all Germans by the Gestapo, who unjustly arrested innocent people, deported them to concentration camps, and confiscated their property. When he spoke these words, his audience knew to whom, among others, he was referring.

In Indonesia in 1991, a German nun prayed for the intersession of Cardinal von Galen, asking him to cure a boy dying of a burst appendix. Without medical intervention, the boy was suddenly and miraculously made well. On October 9, 2005, Clemens August von Galen was declared blessed in a ceremony in Rome presided over by Pope Benedict XVI, a fellow German. His feast day is March 22. The Lion of Munster is a twentieth-century example of how faith and a sense of justice can combine to give men and women the courage to stand up for what is right in the face of the most horrific of evils.

Collect From the Missal of the Sovereign Military Order of Malta

Almighty, ever-living God, by whose gift the Bishop Blessed Clemens August fearlessly defended your glory, the faith of the Church, and the lives of the most vulnerable, grant, by his intercession, that we may always serve you with all our hearts and love others as you have loved them. Through our

Lord Jesus Christ, your Son, who lives and reigns with you in the unity of the Holy Spirit, one God, forever and ever.

14

Blessed Alfredo Ildefonso Schuster

1880–1954

Blessed Ildefonso Schuster, OSB, was born Alfredo Ludovico Schuster in Rome on January 18, 1880 to a father who immigrated to Italy from Bavaria and a mother from Austria's South Tyrol. He died outside Milan at Venegono Seminary on August 30, 1954.

Alfredo's father, Johann, was twice widowed before marrying his mother, Maria Anna Tutzer, who was thirty years younger than her husband. Alfredo had one sister, who entered the Daughters of Charity, and three other half siblings. In a strange incident never fully explained, six-year-old Alfredo was kidnapped off the streets of Rome. He was freed in a matter of hours, and his kidnapper was arrested almost immediately. His father, a master tailor at the Vatican, died in 1889 when Alfredo was nine years old.

Johann's good friend, Baron Pfiffer d'Altishofen, a colonel in the papal Swiss Guard, made young Alfredo's education a priority and arranged for him to attend the Benedictine school attached to the order's monastery at St. Paul's Outside

153

the Wall. A quiet, reserved, and studious boy, young Alfredo excelled in his studies. Taken under the wing of Don Placido Riccardi, Alfredo grew into his vocation, and in 1898 at the age of nineteen, he entered the Benedictine novitiate, taking the religious name of Ildefonso. He professed his first vows in 1900, received his degree in theology and philosophy from the Collegio Pontificio di Sant'Anselmo, and was ordained a priest in 1904.

Schuster was almost immediately entrusted by his Benedictine superiors with significant responsibilities, likely attesting to his serious and mature character. He became master of novices in 1908, an important post in the monastery, which he held until 1916. In that same year, he assumed the role of prior. In 1918, he was elected abbot of the monastery at St. Paul's Outside the Wall. During his years as abbot, he was given papal appointments as rector of the Pontifical Oriental, as consultor to the Congregation of Rites and Congregation for Oriental Churches, and as apostolic visitor to seminaries in Lombardy, Calabria, and Campania. He was seen as a scholarly, prayerful, and patient superior, always academically inclined but with a strong interest in liturgical issues, the plight of the working classes, and evangelization.

During this period, Schuster displayed a wide-ranging understanding of the issues confronting the Italian Church, issues that he would revisit from 1929 to 1954 as cardinal archbishop of Milan. His later ecumenism arose, in part, from his strong interest in the liturgy and history of the Oriental churches. Recognized as an expert in these fields, Pope Pius X named him the consulter to the academic journal *Roma e L'Oriente*, and Benedict XV appointed him a professor and then president of the Pontificio Istituto Orientale. His interests in the study of prayer and sacred music informed his views on the liturgy, which he enthusiastically pursued both as abbot and archbishop.

On February 2, 1922, the archbishop of Milan, Cardinal Achille Ratti, who had been raised to the see of Milan only the year before, was elected pope. He was a librarian by profession and had served from 1907 to 1914 as the prefect of the Ambrosian Library in Milan and subsequently from 1915 to 1921 as prefect of the Vatican library. The beginning years of Ratti's papacy coincided with Schuster's abbotship, and they were very turbulent years for Italian society.

Wracked by street violence between Fascists and Communists, the 1922 Liberal government of Prime Minister Luigi Facta was unable to stem the rampant political violence. Seeing an opportunity to strike a final blow to the crumbling Italian democracy, Benito Mussolini's Fascists staged their infamous March on Rome when Facta's government was just eight months old. When King Victor Emmanuel II refused to sign a declaration of martial law to stop the Fascists, Facta's government resigned, paving the way for Mussolini to take power. By 1925, Mussolini had outlawed political parties, including the Catholic Partito Popolare Italiano (PPI), and was well on his way to consolidating power in the hands of the Fascist government.

The rise of Mussolini initially created confusion and sowed dissension among Italian Catholics. Many Catholics supported the Partito Popolare, an avowed enemy of the Fascist movement. The PPI's politicians and supporters suffered considerable violence at the hands of the Fascists, including serious clashes in the 1920s between Catholic and Fascist university students. During the 1920s, Pius XI offered lukewarm support for the Catholic political movement but strenuously defended the rights of the lay organization of Catholic Action against Fascist hostility and encroachment. It was only in 1928, as the possibility of peace between Church and state emerged, that the harsh rhetoric between the Vatican and Mussolini's government began to abate (Wolff 1990).

As a well-known Benedictine abbot, Schuster generally reflected the official position of the Vatican during these years. He spoke out against the political violence of the period and defended Catholic Action. When Mussolini and Pius XI signed the Lateran Accords in 1929, Schuster, like the Vatican, the Italian hierarchy, and most Catholics, welcomed the end of the long-standing acrimony between Church and state. Named archbishop of Milan by Pius in June 1929, shortly after the signing of the Lateran Accords, Schuster became the first bishop to swear allegiance before King Victor Emanuel in conformity with the obligations of the new treaty.

An uneasy peace reigned between the Fascist state and the Vatican until 1931 when, in what the Vatican perceived as a violation of the Lateran Accords, Mussolini sought to weaken, if not eliminate, the Church's influence in education. He took aim at Catholic Action, claiming that it protected anti-Fascists and surreptitiously undermined Fascist training of the youth. The debate on the role of the Church in education had been roiling Italian politics since the immediate aftermath of the signing of the Lateran Accords.

The government gradually began to countenance violence against Catholic Action and Catholic youth organizations, and within two years of the signing of the accords, open warfare over the control of education had broken out between Pius and Mussolini. The pope responded with a fiery condemnation of Mussolini and Fascism in the encyclical *Non Abbiamo Bisogno*, but by 1931, both sides had concluded they would have to compromise. Catholic Action survived, but in a weakened state, and a brief period of accommodation ensued (Wolff 1990).

The archbishop of Milan was entirely supportive of the Holy See during the crisis of 1931. He was outspoken in his defense of Catholic rights in education and critical of the violent attacks on Catholic youth movements. This is important to note because in the ensuing years of relative accommodation between Fascists and Catholics (1932–1938), Cardinal Schuster was criticized for appearing publicly with government officials on national holidays and for blessing Fascist banners on those occasions. He did so, for example, when Italian troops were sent off to invade Ethiopia in 1935. Because of this, some political elements accused him of being a clerical fascist. Schuster was aware of these criticisms. In 1939, he said that in previous years, he had acknowledged the benefits to the Church of the Lateran Accords and fulfilled his ceremonial duties and spiritual obligations as archbishop of Milan, but he also pointed out that he had strenuously objected to Fascist attempts to control society and the youth. In a 1939 speech, he portrayed Fascism as antithetical to Christianity (Rumi and Majo 1996). "Among us, the Catholic Church today finds itself confronting, not so much a new Fascist state—this already existed in the year of the Concordat [1929]—but confronting a prevailing philosophical-religious system . . . which is the implicit denial of the Apostle's Creed, of the spiritual transcendence of religion, [and] of the rights of the Christian family and the individual."

The Order of Malta made the cardinal a bailiff in 1933. Notably, this was after the crisis of 1931 during which Schuster had acquitted himself well. By this time, Schuster was seen by Mussolini's government as "notoriously anti-Fascist." He opposed the Pact of Steel, Italy's alliance with Nazi Germany. His sharply worded sermon from the pulpit of the Duomo condemning the 1938 Italian racial laws discriminating against the Jews demonstrated his open antipathy towards the regime. The homily was published two days later by the newspaper *L'Italia*, giving it wide circulation beyond Milan. By the time Italy had entered World War II on the side of the Germans, Cardinal Schuster was regarded as an outspoken critic of the Fascist regime.

During the war years, Schuster publicly protested attempts to deport Jews to concentration camps. In 1943 and 1944, the cardinal arranged for scores of Jewish families to take refuge in convents as they made their ways to the safety of Switzerland. In December 1945, with Mussolini's German-supported Republic of Salò collapsing, Schuster attempted to broker an agreement between the Resistance and the Duce. Concerned about the possibility of destructive urban warfare on the streets of Milan, Schuster tried to persuade Mussolini to surrender and repent his sins. The cardinal, who displayed on these discussions his well-known virtues—piety, humility, courage, and patience—spoke one-on-one with the dictator for three hours. In the end, he failed, and Mussolini chose to flee to Como where he met his bloody end at the hands of the partisans.

The postwar years saw Cardinal Schuster embark upon prodigious efforts to relieve the rampant poverty and to recover from the widespread destruction wrought by the war. With homeless dying on the wintry streets of Milan, Schuster took the lead in building apartment complexes on the city periphery, called Domus Ambrosiano, which housed thousands of working class and poor families. His concerns in the postwar years centered on aiding refugees, securing the rights of prisoners, and aiding the poor with a steady stream of basic necessities.

He saw the reconstruction of Italy not only in economic terms but also as a necessary spiritual renewal. He founded a movement to promote better training and culture among the clergy and another to encourage the laity to work with priests throughout the archdiocese. Well before Vatican II (1962–1965), Schuster, the expert liturgist, suggested that the Mass be celebrated in the vernacular, urged that the language be changed in the Good Friday lament for the Jews, and encouraged ecumenical outreach to other Christian churches and to the Jewish community.

Schuster lived the simple, holy, and reflective life of a true and dedicated son of St. Benedict. Contemporaries marveled at the energy and multiplicity of activities that emanated from this frail-looking, ascetic monk. He took the helm of Italy's largest and most important diocese at a critical juncture and guided it, with humility and courage, through some of the most difficult years in Italian history. His work among refugees, on behalf of the homeless and in support of the poor reflected the values of the Order of Malta that had welcomed him as a member in 1933. He died in 1954 and was mourned as a saintly and holy man by his beloved Milanese. Shuster was succeeded as Milan's archbishop by Giovanni Battista Montini, St. Paul VI.

In 1956, Cardinal Schuster was credited with a miraculous intervention on behalf of a nun with an eye tumor causing her to go blind. After praying at Schuster's tomb, her eyesight was almost immediately restored. In 1957, Archbishop Montini initiated the process for the beatification of his predecessor. The cardinal monk was beatified by Pope John Paul II in May 1996. Blessed Alfredo Ildefonso Schuster's feast day is celebrated on August 30.

Collect From the Missal of the Sovereign Military Order of Malta

Lord God, who gave strength to Blessed Alfredo Ildefonso so that by faith and the practice of good works he could shed luster on the Church and enrich with the example of virtues the flock entrusted to his care as a good shepherd, grant, that by being attentive to his teaching, we may walk securely under the guidance of the Gospel until we behold you in your Kingdom. Through our Lord Jesus Christ, your Son, who lives and reigns with you in the unity of the Holy Spirit, one God, forever and ever.

15

Blessed Vilmos Apor de Altorja

1892–1945

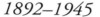

Vilmos Apor was born on February 29, 1892 in Segesvar, Transylvania, then a part of the Austro-Hungarian
Empire. He became a priest during World War I and minis-
tered to the Hungarian people as a pastor and bishop during
the interwar period (1919–1945). He died protecting innocent refugees in 1945, shot by Soviet Russian troops.

Vilmos was born to a noble family that traced its lineage
in Transylvania to the thirteenth century. At the time of
his birth, Transylvania was an eastern province of Hungary
that had been a principality and part of the Crown of St.
Stephen (Hungarian crown) since 1000. Under the Austro-
Hungarian Compromise of 1867, which established the
dual monarchy ruled by the Hapsburg Emperor Franz Josef,
Transylvania lost its autonomous status as a principality and
was directly incorporated into Hungary. Segesvar (Sighisoara
in Romanian), the birthplace of Vilmos, reflected the same
multi-cultural environment that existed in all of Transylvania. Although the town's largest ethnic group was Swabian

(German), it had a significant Hungarian and, to a lesser extent, Romanian population.

Transylvania itself was a large, diverse, multicultural region within the Hapsburg lands. According to the 1910 Hungarian royal census, Hungarian was the first language of residents in thirty of the region's forty-one urban settlements. Ethnic Hungarians, including Transylvania's Hungarian-speaking Jews, made up 32 percent of the total Transylvanian population, while 54 percent were ethnic Romanians and 11 percent ethnic Germans. It could be said that northern Transylvania was the home of most Hungarians, southern Transylvania that of most Romanians, but villages and towns were often a complex mix of ethnicities.

Vilmos's father, Baron Gabor Apor de Altorja, and his mother, Countess Fidelia Palffy, both devout Catholics, were from the region's Hungarian aristocracy. Like all Hungarian nobility, they were fluent in both Hungarian and German and supportive of the Habsburg dynasty. The Apors had a long history of public service. Baron Gabor continued that tradition, serving as the emperor-king's personal representative, or lord lieutenant, to Mures County. Vilmos was the seventh of eight (five survived) children born to the baron and the countess, who was twelve years younger than her husband. When Vilmos was three years old, his father was appointed secretary of state for royal Hungarian affairs by the emperor-king, a role that would bring him into regular contact with the highest government circles in imperial service. In 1895, the Baron moved his family to Vienna, although they kept the manor house near Segesvar.

The Transylvanian baron acquitted himself well with the tireless, detail-oriented Franz Josef, and he was looked upon as a competent and loyal member of the imperial government. However, in 1898 at the age of forty-seven, the baron succumbed to complications from long-term diabetes. Vilmos's widowed mother decided to remain in Vienna with the children, although she made sure that the family returned to Segesvar at least once a year for an extended period. Young Vilmos later remarked how much he anticipated and enjoyed these vacations in Transylvania.

Fatherless at six years old, Vilmos grew very close to his mother, and he shared a special relationship with the countess for the remainder of their lives. He was constantly reminded, however, of the goodness of his father, who "was honoured as one of the leading personalities of Transylvania" and who was remembered for his motto: "Let us forget ourselves for the sake of others" (Nemeth 2011). Guided by his father's memory and his mother's devout Catholicism, Vilmos, by all accounts, had a normal and happy childhood. He stood out in school only for his intelligence and frequent attendance at Mass and Benediction. In 1900, he completed elementary school in Vienna and, at the age of eight, was sent to the Jesuit boarding school in Kalksburg, Austria.

In Kalksburg, where he spent six years, Vilmos was an outstanding student and a good athlete, popular with his classmates. It is said that his years with the Jesuits at Kalksburg exposed him to diverse peoples and broadened his outlook on life. In 1906, adhering to a long-standing family tradition, he was sent to the Jesuit school in Kalocsa, Hungary, to complete high school. Thus, like most nobility of the dual monarchy, Vilmos was equally at ease with the Magyar and German languages and had studied the history and traditions of the empire.

At Kalocsa, again within a supportive Jesuit environment, Vilmos's desire for the priesthood continued to grow. Finally, at the age of sixteen, he spoke to his mother about becoming a priest. At first, Countess Fidelia counseled her son to be patient and reflect further on such a serious decision. The next year, as Christmas approached, Vilmos asked his mother for the one gift that he wanted more than anything: her blessing to go to the seminary. Realizing that Vilmos was intent on becoming a priest, the countess gladly gave her permission. In 1909, he applied to the seminary in the Diocese of Gyor in northwest Hungary where a relative of his, Count Miklos Szechenyi, was the bishop.

Bishop Szechenyi sent Vilmos to study at Innsbruck, where he remained for five years. The young seminarian sought out the Innsbruck Jesuits and took lodgings and classes with them. He eventually completed his doctorate in theology in 1916. In 1911, before his courses at Innsbruck were completed, he transferred from the Diocese of Gyor to the Diocese of Nagyvarad (Oradea Mar) in the Hungarian area of Transylvania, following Bishop Szechenyi who was named its ordinary that same year.

In August 1915, one year after the outbreak of the Great War, Vilmos Apor was ordained a priest. His older brother, Gabor, was at the front and unable to attend, but his mother and sister were granted leave from their Red Cross volunteer work to attend Vilmos's ordination and first Mass. The young priest was assigned to a parish in Gyula, about

147 miles southeast of Budapest. Bishop Szechenyi sent his charge off with words that Father Apor lived by for the rest of his life:

Respect the old, seek the company of your fellow priests, treat ignorant people with toleration, be merciful to the poor, full of pity towards those who suffer, and be kind to sinners. Remain always God's servant, ready to work for him and to make sacrifices. Learn from the Most Sacred Heart of our Lord Jesus Christ to love, endure, suffer, and forgive (O'Driscoll 1993).

Father Apor's diary tells us that he arrived in Gyula brimming with enthusiasm for his assignment and gratitude for his vocation.

In 1917, Bishop Szechenyi asked Vilmos to serve as a military chaplain on a Red Cross hospital train for three months. The young priest was struck by the horrors of the war and the suffering he witnessed firsthand. He returned from this experience to his parish even more eager to continue his work for social justice among the poor and weak. Before he left for his military assignment, Father Apor had established a society for the protection of women in collaboration with the Hungarian Sisters of Social Service. Upon his return to Gyula, he took up this work again, urging all women, married, single, or working, to come to the society with their problems, including helping them find relatives missing in action.

Just as Father Apor was finding his stride again as a parish priest, his bishop sent him to the diocesan seminary to fill a vacant place on the faculty. He went obediently but reluctantly, explaining that he had no desire to become a professor. Rather, he preferred his pastoral work, especially among the poor. Vilmos spent two years at the seminary college and returned to his parish in Gyula in 1919, a year of unprecedented turmoil in the Austro-Hungarian Empire.

The defeat in World War I shattered the dual monarchy into a plethora of successor states, ostensibly based on ethnicity. The Habsburg monarchy, in the person of Emperor Charles I (King Charles IV in Hungary), was overthrown in both the Austrian and Hungarian regions. One after another, the dual monarchy's myriad of ethnicities threw off the rule of Austria and Hungary, establishing new kingdoms and republics. The vast expanse of Central and East Europe, for hundreds of years held together by the supranational scepter of the Habsburgs, was now comprised of small, squabbling states based on nationality.

Hungary went through a serious crisis at the end of the war as the Bolshevik party of Bela Kun took control of the country in 1919, provoking a strong and violent reaction from the country's nobility, commercial classes, and peasantry, called the "White Terror." The Romanian army, now on the victorious side of the war, entered Budapest to stamp out the communist menace, and a royal government of Hungary was formed with Admiral Nicholas Horthy as regent for the exiled King Charles. In 1920, the newly constituted government was compelled to sign the Treaty of Trianon, stripping Hungary of two-thirds of its territory and creating widespread resentment throughout the kingdom.

By the terms of the treaty, all of Transylvania was lost to Romania, including Szegesvar, ancient seat of the Apor family, which became known as Sighisoara. Vast territories, mostly historical lands of the Crown of St. Stephen, in the north and east were ceded to Poland and Romania and in the south and southwest to Serbia and Italy. New states were carved out of the fallen carcass of the Habsburg Empire, such as Czechoslovakia and Yugoslavia. Millions of ethnic groups found themselves cut off from their conationals by new boundaries, creating an irredentist problem of major proportions in almost every successor state.

In Hungary, the single most important foreign policy goal in the interwar period was to regain the historic lands that had been lost with the Treaty of Trianon. In domestic politics, the country remained in a semi-feudal state, dominated by aristocratic landowners, with uneven electoral suffrage, and an economy overly dependent on agriculture. By and large, the Hungarian aristocracy held fairly homogeneous political and social views, and the Catholic hierarchy was almost entirely drawn from the nobility. With few notable exceptions, this worldview was aggressively irredentist, committed to a hierarchical social system, extremely anti-Bolshevik, and somewhat anti-Semitic.

In this environment, Father Apor became the pastor of his parish and spent the next twenty-three years, until 1941, in Gyula. There he worked diligently to implement the social teaching of Popes Leo XIII and Pius XI, assisting the working class and peasants and promoting lay involvement in transforming society through Catholic Action. Like the popes, Father Apor saw the dangers of the left (socialism) and the right (fascism), from East (Bolshevism) and the West (unfettered capitalism). When later, as bishop of Gyor, he called for the distribution of Church farmland to poor sharecroppers and expressed his willingness to start with the extensive landholdings of his diocese, the primate, Cardinal Jusztinian Seredi, and many conservative Catholic politicians said this time he "had gone too far."

He sought out the poorest of his flock, and when the large public housing projects were built around the city without churches or priests, Father Apor went, in good Jesuit fashion, to "meet the people where they were." For fourteen years, he brought the sacraments, spiritual guidance, and economic assistance to people living in these projects. In 1935, he established a day care center in the Mariafalva project to help working parents care for their children. The next year, he offered his services to the Catholic Agrarian Young Men's Council. The organization grew rapidly with his guidance. He may well have lived a full life of prayer, service to his parishioners, care for the poor, and Jesuit retreats in Budapest and been quite satisfied. However, it was not to be so simple for Father Apor, as Hungary, Europe, and the world barreled ahead into a second great war.

In 1938, the Hungarian government, following the lead of Hitler's regime, instituted a series of three discriminatory laws aimed at the Jewish population. The first of these limited the number of Jews permitted in the various professions without distinguishing between baptized and non-baptized views. The law was introduced the same year that Pius XI issued his encyclical, *Mit Brenender Sorge*, condemning Nazi racial theory. The Hungarian bishops, who were members of Parliament's Upper House, opposed the inclusion of Christian Jews in the law, objected to the racial approach to the "Jewish question," and complained that collective deprivation of human rights was immoral. However, after a riotous parliamentary debate, the bishops voted, despite misgivings, for the legislation. Assured by Prime Minister Pal Teleki that passing the bill would dent the worrisome and growing German appeal within Hungary and "take the wind out of the Nazi's sails," the bishops ultimately went along.

The second Jewish law in 1939 curtailed the citizenship rights of Jews, again making no distinction between baptized and non-baptized Jews. The bishops again protested this language in the bill and added that non-baptized Jews who had adopted Hungarian culture and mores should also be exempted. It does not appear as if historians have unearthed any comment by Father Apor on the first and second Jewish laws that were enacted before he became a bishop.

The third Jewish law was enacted in 1941, the same year that Hungary entered World War II on the side of the Germans and Vilmos Apor was named bishop of Gyor, a large diocese in the northwest of the country, bordering on Austria and Slovakia. This law expanded the definition of a Jew and forbade marriages between Jews and Gentiles, regardless of whether the former were converts to Christianity. Bishops and priests roundly criticized this legislation and this time largely refused to vote for it. As a relatively new bishop installed only in March 1941, Bishop Apor apparently did not issue any public statements opposing the legislation, but he quickly involved himself in the Holy Cross Society headed by outspoken Archbishop Gyula Zichy, which focused on supporting and protecting baptized Jews. His dedication to this work was recognized when in 1942, upon the death of Archbishop Zichy, Bishop Apor was asked to take his place.

With the Holy Cross Society as his platform, Bishop Apor attempted to alleviate the predicament of the Jewish people, who made up 6.1 percent of Hungary's population. In a 1942 letter to the prime minister, he vigorously argued that baptized Jews should be exempt from all restrictions and that racial origins were outweighed in importance by an individual's spiritual attitude. He objected to the forced use of yellow stars in public to identify Jews, and he wrote to the cardinal primate urging him to use his influence with the government to alleviate the dire conditions of Jewish Christians, who numbered about one hundred thousand nation-wide.

Believing that baptized Jews may have had a better chance of avoiding persecution than others, Bishop Apor streamlined the conversion process to provide Jews more rapidly with documentation proving that they were Christians. He authorized baptisms within days of completing a few basic classes on Christianity. These classes were often packed with fifty to one hundred converts each, all hoping that baptismal certificates would afford them some level of protection from the growing Nazi terror. He also began to speak out publicly against the racial laws and the influence of Nazism within Hungary.

In 1944, when the Jews in Gyor itself were forced into a ghetto, Apor angrily addressed the minister of interior, Andor Jaross, criticizing the establishment of the Jewish Ghetto as a "shocking injustice." He went on: "I protest before God, Hungary and the world, against this measure which is in contradiction to human rights and punishes not only innocent adults, against whom no legal action has been taken, but also children incapable of committing a crime" (O'Driscoll 1993).

Six times Bishop Apor requested permission to visit the ghetto to bring food, clothing, and medicine. Six times the authorities refused. The Hungarian government eventually succumbed to pressure from Germany to round up Jews for extermination. In March 1944, the Germans forced Horthy to install as prime minister Dome Sztojay, a Nazi sympathizer, who immediately ordered the deportation of Jews to the death camps.

With the German military holding sway in Hungary, a Nazi-inspired national government, and the rounding up of Hungarian Jews underway, several of the bishops persuaded the primate, Cardinal Jusztinian Seredi, to draft a joint pastoral letter in conjunction with Protestant groups. Bishop Apor, citing the calamity facing the Jews, asked the primate to "resort to extreme measures in opposition to the government" and to "take energetic action." To his fellow bishop Jozsef Petery of Vac, Apor wrote, "One cannot tolerate anti-Semitism. It must be condemned. . . . It is not enough to be sorry for those who are persecuted . . . one must state openly that no one may be punished for the blood in his veins. . . . What the Jews are undergoing is genocide" (O'Driscoll 1993).

The pastoral letter from all the bishops, with the primate at their head, was entitled "Successor to the Apostles." It was ready for clandestine dissemination throughout Hungary by late June 1944. The letter specifically rejected racism, calling on the government to stop the persecution of people based on their racial origin. The bishops accused the government of ignoring all their previous protests and called on it to "respect divine law and remedy injustices at once." The letter warns the government that its "illegal" actions, if not halted, in this time of national crisis would surely "bring God's wrath upon his people."

In the days just before the scheduled release of the pastoral letter, it was somehow seen by the government. The minister of justice met with the primate, begging him to quash its distribution. The primate, who was cautious by nature and had been pushed by the bishops into sanctioning the pastoral letter, gave two conditions for its suppression: first, that the deportation of Jews out of the country stop immediately; second, that enforcement of the Jewish laws be suspended. Fearful of the social unrest the letter might provoke, the government, after intense negotiations, essentially agreed to those terms. The distribution of the pastoral letter was aborted, but several bishops were not pleased. Apor wrote to the primate: "I very much regret the postponement of the publication of a joint pastoral letter concerning the Jewish problem."

In the end, the Germans, furious at Horthy's two failed attempts to take Hungary out of the war, invaded its ally in March 1944. Under the Nazi-installed fascist government of the Arrow Cross, the deportations continued, with Eichmann himself spending time in Hungary overseeing the transports. It is estimated that of the almost 850,000 Jews living in Hungary in 1940, only 255,000 survived in 1946. Bishop Apor had accurately named the "resettlement policy" what it was: genocide (Wolff and Hoensch 1987).

Amid the political and social turmoil of the war years, Bishop Apor redoubled his efforts on behalf of those in need. The bishop's country villa and his palace in Gyor were periodically filled with refugees and hidden Jews. In the palace, there were a considerable number of people holed up in the cellar where the bishop would say Mass for them. As the fighting approached western Hungary and Hungarian authorities urged the population to evacuate, Bishop Apor encouraged his priests and religious to remain at their posts. "A servant abandons his flock and runs away," he wrote to them, "the good shepherd gives his life for his sheep."

Bishop Apor, admired for his judgment and rectitude, was also in the forefront of planning for a more just and democratic government after the war was over. In the summer of 1943, he hosted a clandestine meeting of leaders of Catholic lay movements, including the agrarian youth league, with five hundred thousand members and the Association of Catholic Urban Workers. Believing that the Germans would ultimately lose the war, the participants outlined two major goals: 1, to support the Horthy government in its efforts to withdraw from the war and the German alliance; 2, to begin to prepare for the transition from a feudal oligarchy to a liberal democratic state.

By March 29, 1945, the Russian army had entered Gyor, and drunken and poorly disciplined Red troops began to loot stores and homes and abuse Hungarian women. The first contingent of Russians approached the bishop's palace looking to take young women away with them to work in kitchens. Apor, surmising the Russians' real intentions, asked the elderly men and women refugees to volunteer for kitchen duty while he hid the young women refugees within the palace.

Shortly afterwards, a group of five inebriated soldiers arrived at the bishop's residence and spotted a young woman who had come out of hiding. The Russians chased her down near the entrance to the cellar. Hearing her screams, Apor raced to her side and ordered the soldiers out of the palace. At first, they sullenly turned and walked away, but then one of them wheeled around and fired his machine gun, hitting Bishop Apor with three bullets. It was Good Friday 1945. Bishop Apor was taken by stretcher through the chaotic city streets to the hospital. There he underwent an unsuccessful operation, dying from his wounds on Easter Monday.

Conservative by nature, Blessed Vilmos Apor came from an old aristocratic Hungarian family with deeps roots in Transylvania. In fact, his connections were so strong in the highest circles that in 1919 he was able to travel to Bucharest to meet with Queen Mary to request successfully the release of captured Hungarian officers. His ancestral home in Segesvar was lost to the Romanians in 1920. He was a legitimist and supported the return of the Habsburgs to the throne of St. Stephen. Given all this, one would think that he would be the embodiment of a mid-twentieth century, reactionary Hungarian noble. But he wasn't.

Apor did share the irredentist views of the overwhelming majority of interwar Hungarians, but he parted company with most all Hungarian bishops when he spoke up for agrarian reform, arguing that the Church, one of the largest landholders in the kingdom, should lease its farmland to peasant small holders. Nor did most bishops share his commitment to social justice and the poor, and he found himself with only a few other colleagues at his side when he spoke out against the treatment of the Jews. Indeed, it could be said that he led the primate on this issue rather than the other way around. In these respects Vilmos Apor stood out as a man of heroic virtue, even before he gave his life to save a woman from certain sexual abuse.

In November 1946, the cause for Bishop Apor's canonization was started by his successor in Gyor, and in 1947, the primate, Cardinal Jozsef Mindszenty, agreed to forward the cause to Rome. On November 9, 1997, Vilmos Apor de Altorja, bishop and martyr, was beatified by Pope John Paul II in St. Peter's Square. His feast day is on May 23. He was a conventual chaplain ad honorum in the Order of Malta.

Collect From the Missal of the Sovereign Military Order of Malta

Almighty and ever-living God, with the help of your grace, Bishop William merited the crown of martyrdom by courageously shedding his blood for his flock. Grant that the difficulties of daily life may not hinder us from doing your will and that we may offer our service for the salvation of our neighbors. Through Our Lord Jesus Christ, your Son, who lives and reigns with you in the unity of the Holy Spirit, one God, forever and ever.

Pope St. John XXIII

1881–1963

A ngelo Giuseppe Roncalli was born to a peasant family of sharecroppers on November 25, 1881 in the small village of Sotto il Monte, ten miles from the town of Bergamo. He was the fourth child (first boy) of thirteen children. He died in Rome on June 3, 1963.

The Roncalli family life was typical of the village of Sotto il Monte: devout, simple, dominated by work and the rituals of the Church. From an early age, Angelo was drawn to the priesthood. He once said that "he could never remember a time when he didn't want to be a priest." Encouraged by his Uncle Zaverio and his parish priest, Don Rebuzzi, he entered the minor seminary at the age of ten. Although he left home at an early age, Angelo never lost his strong attachment to his family.

The Bergamo seminary was very strict. No newspapers were permitted, proper behavior and modesty were strictly enforced, and contact with the outside world was carefully circumscribed and monitored. Roncalli was a "serious-minded, intense, scrupulous" seminarian. He began his diary in these years, and it presents a picture of a young man intent on becoming a good priest. While at the seminary, he developed his own "rules of life" that he practiced until his death: a strict regime of daily prayer, Mass, devotions, meditation, reflections, and invocations.

In 1901, Angelo was sent by his bishop to the Roman College to further his studies. In Rome, Angelo chose history as his concentration and quickly excelled in his coursework. His journal reveals a happy and contented young man, confident of his own intellectual abilities but sometimes pained by feelings of social inferiority. He was ordained in Rome in 1903, his parents and Uncle Zaverio absent, as they could not afford the train fare from Sotto il Monte. Roncalli celebrated his first Mass at the Crypt of St. Peter.

From 1904 to 1914, he was secretary to the progressive bishop Giacomo Radini Tedeschi, whom Roncalli dubbed "my bishop." It was an important learning experience for the young priest, increasing his exposure to Christian democracy and service to the poor. At Bergamo, Roncalli also began to teach history. His scholarship and social activism brought him perilously close to running afoul of the Vatican's anti-Modernist crusade, but he was careful not to cross the line into "error." In 1914, Roncalli's bishop died, and a year later, the young priest was drafted into the Italian army. He spent the war as a medic tending to the wounded in a Bergamo hospital. When he was finally mustered out in 1918, he "burnt his uniform, glad to be rid of it."

In the Italian post-war political turmoil, Roncalli became a strong supporter of the Catholic Popular Party in its struggle against both the communists and fascists. He began to travel in Popolari, anti-fascist circles and soon met a young priest, Giovanni Battista Montini, later Pope Paul VI. The twenty-three-year-old Montini was beginning his apostolate to the university students, and he invited Roncalli to speak to them. It was the beginning of a long friendship, joined from the very beginning by a common political viewpoint, a strong anti-fascist bent, and a belief in social activity among the workers and poor, making a common cause, if necessary, with socialists and communists.

In 1925, Roncalli was posted to the Vatican diplomatic corps. His first assignment was to Bulgaria as apostolic visitor. Some observers felt that Roncalli was shipped off to Bulgaria by Vatican conservatives because of his vocal support of the Popular Party. In any case, now an archbishop, Roncalli spent ten years in Bulgaria. As a diplomat, he was a success, but Bulgaria, with very few Catholics, was not an important posting. However, Roncalli did learn a great deal about the Orthodox. In 1935, he was transferred to Istanbul, a nod to his growing reputation as an expert on the Balkans and Orthodoxy.

As apostolic delegate in neutral Turkey during World War II, Archbishop Roncalli had to walk a fine line between the Allies and the Axis powers. Roncalli was also responsible for Greece, and his actions during the Nazi occupation ranged from attempting to persuade the Soviet Union to provide POW information to intervening to assist Jews destined for deportation. Of the plight of the Jews, he wrote, "Poor children of Israel. Daily I hear their groans around me. They are relatives and fellow countrymen of Jesus." He used his good offices with the king of Bulgaria to help Jews in danger of being sent to concentration camps and intervened in Hungary and Romania to stop deportations (Malouf 2008).

In 1944, at the age of sixty-three, Archbishop Roncalli was sent to Paris as nuncio. In France, the new nuncio was thrown into the post-war controversies surrounding worker-priests, cooperation with communists, and the Vatican's suspicion of "historicism" in theological studies. Roncalli steered clear of major controversies, but he was sympathetic to the worker-priests and to new ways of reaching the working classes. Further, his historical training put him firmly in the camp of the new scholarship. In 1953, Pius XII named Roncalli patriarch of Venice, his first pastoral responsibility in over thirty years. At seventy-one, Roncalli believed that this would be the final responsibility of his life.

In Venice, the new patriarch was dismayed by the contrast between the city's great wealth and abject poverty. He was concerned that the Vatican policy of uncompromising anti-communism was pushing Christian democracy to the right. By reducing every election to a struggle between communism and Catholicism, Roncalli believed that Christian democracy was forgetting its commitment to social justice. In Venice, Roncalli took up the role of conciliator between rich and poor, Catholic and communist, worker and professional, and fascist and anti-fascist. He reached out to the Socialist Party and deplored the gap between Christian and secular society, remarks that did not go unnoticed by Vatican conservatives.

In 1956, Roncalli was invested in the Order of Malta as a baliff. His strong emphasis on care for the poor and his international outlook made him an ideal candidate for order. At the time, the order was in the midst of a serious crisis of governance. With the tacit approval of Pope Pius XII, Cardinal Nicola Canali, aided by Cardinal Francis Spellman and Cardinal Giuseppe Pizzardo, attempted to take control of the order upon the death of Grand Master Chigi in 1951. Canali succeeded in preventing the election of a new grand master and establishing a cardinals' commission to investigate the order. He and his allies formed a majority on the commission. When the first commission failed in its objective to place Canali in the vacant chair of the grand master, the pope was persuaded to establish in 1954 a second cardinals' commission again comprised of Canali and his allies, thus continuing the effort to subordinate the order to the Vatican bureaucracy.

In 1955, an election was held to replace the lieutenant, Antonio Hercolani, who led the order in the absence of a grand master. At the insistence of the commission, the election was for another lieutenant, not grand master. Canali's candidate was soundly defeated, which weakened the cardinals' cause. On October 9, 1958, Pius XII died. On October 28, on the eleventh ballot, Angelo Cardinal Roncalli was elected pope, taking the name John.

With the death of Pius and the papacy of Roncalli, the siege of the order was lifted. Canali and his allies soon found themselves sidelined by the new pope's progressive agenda, and the cardinals' commission was, once and for all, dissolved. On June 24, 1961, Pope John approved a revised version of the order's constitution in the apostolic bull *Exigit Apostolicum officum*, recognizing its historic privileges and characteristics and reaffirming the religious life of its professed.

Although Pope John loved tradition, he nevertheless wanted a more human and accessible papacy. His first words as pope dwelled on the pastoral role of the pope, and he referred to himself as his flock's brother. He made it clear that he valued catechesis more than magisterium. The difference, he said, was that while magisterium lectures the world from the outside, catechesis takes people where they are and seeks to ground the Gospel in the thick of human life. His Christmas visit to a Roman prison and his embracing of a convicted murderer underscored for the world that this pope would be a pastor above all (Cahill 2002).

In January 1959, the pope announced his intention to summon an ecumenical council. Montini remarked to a friend, "This holy old boy doesn't realize the hornet's nest that he's stirring up." But misgivings aside, Montini was a major supporter of the council as a means of renewal and reform. John set forth the council's goals: to help the Church, in conformity with tradition, bring its teachings and discipline up to date, to renew the religious life of Catholics, and to seek the unity of all Christians. The council was to be a pastoral event, a celebration of faith, not a vehicle to condemn the errors of the modem world.

On the eve of the council, Montini wrote, "We shall have a Council of positive rather than punitive reforms, and of exhortation rather than anathemas." At one point in reviewing preliminary drafts, Pope John measured a page with his ruler and said, "Seven inches of condemnations and one of praise! Is that the way to talk to the modern world?" In the pope's view, anathemas were not the answer to the errors of the contemporary world. Upon hearing this, conservative cardinal Alfredo Ottaviani was overheard to say, "I pray God that I may die before the end of the Council. In that way I can at least die a Catholic" (Hebblethwaite 1993).

John was suffering from stomach cancer even before the first session of the council began, and he did not live to see his great initiative through. Apart from the council, his most noteworthy legacies were his encyclicals, *Mater et magistri* and *Pacem in terris*. In the former, John endorsed the concept of a modern welfare state, supporting cooperatives and trade unions. In the latter, he insisted upon freedom of conscience, peace, and protection of fundamental human rights. He also criticized imperialism and set the Church's sights on the problems of the developing world. John finished *Pacem in terris* only months before he died in June 1963. His last words, spoken twice in succession, were: "Lord, you know that I love you."

Angelo Roncalli, pope and bailiff of the Order of Malta, was proclaimed a saint on April 27, 2014. His feast day is October 11, commemorating the opening of Vatican II. He is attributed with one miracle thus far: the curing of an Italian nun, Sister Caterina Capitani, of stomach cancer. Although his body was uncorrupted when exhumed, the Vatican attributed this to the embalming method and the seal of the casket, not to a miraculous event. In the case of John, Pope Francis waived the need for a second miracle for sainthood, citing *certascientia*, or "sure knowledge," of his holiness.

Collect From the Missal of the Sovereign
Military Order of Malta

Almighty, ever-living God, who in Pope Saint John, have given a living example of Christ, the Good Shepherd, to shine throughout the earth, grant us, we pray, that through his intercession, we may joyfully pour out an abundance of Christian charity. Through our Lord Jesus Christ, your Son, who lives and reigns with you in the unity of the Holy Spirit, one God, forever and ever.

17

Pope St. Paul VI

1897–1978

Pope St. Paul VI was born Giovanni Battista Montini on September 26, 1897 to devout upper-class parents in the northern city of Brescia in Italy. He died in Castel Gandolfo, Italy on August 6, 1978.

From childhood, Battista, as Montini was known, was steeped in the Catholic social activism of his parents, Giorgio and Giudetta. His father was a prominent lawyer, editor of an important Catholic newspaper, and an anti-fascist deputy representing Brescia in the national Parliament. His mother served as the national president of the Union of Catholic Women. Both were well-known members of Don Luigi Sturzo's Partito Popolare Italiano, with excellent contacts within the Vatican.

Battista was educated by Jesuits, entered the seminary in Brescia, and was ordained in 1920. He was a slightly built young man, never in very robust health. In fact, he spent many months of his seminary studies working from home due to his physical frailty. Always an excellent student, he was sent to Rome to study at the Vatican's school of diplomacy, the prestigious Accademia dei Nobili Ecclesiatici, and was posted to the nunciature in Warsaw for a brief time before returning to Rome to work in the Secretariat of State.

During the Fascist years (1922–1943), Montini served as the chaplain to the national association of Catholic university students where he met and befriended many future Christian Democratic politicians and prime ministers. While working with the students, he met a young priest from Bergamo, Don Angelo Roncalli (later Pope John XXIII), and the two became lifelong friends. They both received red hats in the 1950s, Montini from the hand of Roncalli himself, and they both wore the red shoes of the fisherman.

Concerned in the 1930s about an increasingly repressive Fascist regime that was drawing closer to Hitler and his racial theories, Montini carefully steered the university students away from Fascism without repercussions from Mussolini's regime. While Montini may have been cautious and discreet in public, there was nothing subtle about his private criticisms of the Fascist dictatorship (Wolff 1990). All the while, he also served as the Vatican's undersecretary of state to Cardinal Eugene Pacelli (later Pope Pius XII).

During the Second World War, Montini surrounded himself with anti-fascists and dissidents to such an extent that the Italian Fascists accused him of being anti-Italian and pro-Allied. Inside the Vatican, cardinals sympathetic to Mussolini worked against him. But during war, Pope Pius XII never wavered in his support for Montini, protecting him from the conservative wing within the Curia (Wolff 1986, 1990).

Montini became a member of the Order of Malta in 1937, entering as a knight of magistral grace. In 1938, he was awarded the Grand Cross. He entered the order in the midst of his activism with students, his concern for the poor, and his involvement in the difficult domestic and international political situation of the times. Much like his parents, his focus on social justice placed him in the progressive wing of Catholicism. The Order of Malta's emphasis on serving the poor and sick must have been attractive to Montini who, both in his youth and as pope, rallied to the side of the poor and encouraged others to follow suit.

Upon the death of Cardinal Alfredo Ildefonso Schuster in 1954, Pope Pius named Montini archbishop of Milan. This appointment was seen by some inside the Vatican as a demotion of sorts. Montini's support of the progressive social justice oriented worker-priest movement and his opposition to a Catholic electoral alliance with the conservative right-wing parties caused him to fall from favor inside the Vatican. Finally vanquished by his conservative enemies in the curia, Montini left Rome for Milan and its 3.5 million Catholics, 1,000 churches and 3,500 priests. In Milan, Archbishop Montini reached out to workers and the poor, opened dialogue with non-Catholics, sought modern communications vehicles to reach people of all walks of life, and welcomed artists, intellectuals, and writers to his residence (Hebblethwaite 1993). In 1956, Montini was made a bailiff grand cross of the Order of Malta.

When his friend, Angelo Roncalli, was elected pope in 1958, the first red hat that he dispensed was to the archbishop of Milan, Giovanni Battista Montini. Cardinal

Montini played a critical role in the planning and preparation for the Second Vatican Council, and he was viewed as one of the pope's closest collaborators. When John died in June 1963, Montini was considered a leading candidate to succeed his friend as pope.

Cardinal Montini was elected pope on June 21, 1963 during the uncompleted Second Vatican Council. Taking the name Paul VI, the new pope faced a growing divide in the council deliberations between conservative and progressive prelates. His approach to the remaining two council sessions was to support the progressive majority while at the same time ensuring that the rights of the conservative minority were respected. To the chagrin of the traditionalists, Paul championed collegiality and established the synod of bishops; he mediated the issue of religious liberty in favor of the progressives and launched the practical methods to realize John XXIII's ecumenical dream. At the same time, he angered liberals by his unwavering support for the primacy of the pope and clerical celibacy, his prohibition of birth control, and his unilateral establishment of Mary as "Mother of the Church."

In certain ways, Paul's entire papacy was a grand and precarious effort to lead the Church in a time of great change and turmoil without permanently alienating either traditional or progressive Catholics. His five encyclicals reflected this approach, ranging from the call for renewal and dialogue within the Church (*Ecclesiam suam* 1964) to his reinforcement of traditional teachings on the Eucharist (*Mysterium fidei* 1965) and celibacy (*Sacerdotalis caelibatus* 1967). In *Populorum progessio* (1967), Paul focused on human development and criticized the divide between the rich and poor nations. He pointed out the shortcomings of the free market as a cure for poverty and called for "global solidarity." In *Humanae vitae* (1968), the pope's eloquent defense of human life was reduced by the world's media into a simplistic condemnation of artificial birth control. The negative reaction that it evoked among the liberal and secular press so stunned the pope that he never again, in the ten remaining years of his pontificate, issued another encyclical.

Nonetheless, Paul consistently called on Catholics and others to choose "the preferential option for the poor," which reflected the call of the Gospels and the spirit of Vatican II. His historic speech at the United Nations condemned war and called upon cooperation between communist and capitalist nations. His Ostpolitik initiative towards Eastern Europe's communist bloc sought better diplomatic relations to improve the lot of Catholics in these countries. Ahead of his time, he was convinced that communist domination of Europe was a passing phenomenon and that the Church must prepare for the future of free, democratic Eastern European states. At the time, however, conservatives saw his policy as a "sell out" to communist tyrants. The pope used the concessions that Ostpolitik brought him from Eastern bloc nations to appoint like-minded bishops, such as Karol Wojtyla (later Pope John Paul II), who would eventually play a significant role in the fall of communism in Europe.

The pope's travels often took him to the developing world where his focus on justice, peace, and social reform was generally well received. He often remarked publicly, "If you want peace, seek justice." In 1968, Paul's appearance in Medellin,

Colombia at the Latin American bishop's conference reinforced the Church's preferential option for the poor. Paul's support and elevation of key "liberation theology" bishops, such as Helder Camara, Aloisio Lorsheider, and Paolo Evaristo Arns, gave impetus to a "third way" of development in Latin America, led by the Church, between communism and capitalism. Although Paul was admired in many circles for his openness to such initiatives, he was much criticized by conservative elements of society. His launching of the World Peace Day project on January 1, 1968, with the support of the United Nations, and his brokering the Vietnam peace talks underscored his sustained and vocal opposition to war.

These concerns for peace, justice, and modernity were reflected in the pope's brief address to the leadership of the Order of Malta assembled in Rome in October 1970 for a chapter general. He praised the order for its work with the poor and its struggle for social justice in the developing world. Citing Vatican II, he encouraged the assembled knights to "make adjustments according to the needs of the time and place . . . [and] resort to suitable techniques, including modern ones, and abandon whatever activities are today less in keeping with the spirit of community and its authentic character."

In the United States and Europe, Paul filled episcopal vacancies with pastoral priests who would support the implementation of the Second Vatican Council's decrees. He also sought to "internationalize" the curia and the college of cardinals, putting a mandatory retirement age on cardinals eligible to vote in a papal election. With the purpose of promoting vigor and dialogue with the world, he extended the mandatory retirement age to bishops as well. But his message of peace and social justice was often overwhelmed in the First World by controversies around the flight from religious life, the new Mass, women in the Church, sexual mores, and birth control.

In the latter years of Montini's papacy, Catholicism seemed wracked by fissures between right and left, traditionalists and progressives. Paul, who suffered immensely from these conflicts, nevertheless stayed the course that he chose when he ascended the papal throne in 1963. He never hesitated to implement the social, theological, and liturgical reforms of Vatican II, but he never went beyond them either. In effect, he supported the progressive majority within Catholicism and ensured the rights of the conservative minority. He passed anathema on no one, not even his most vocal enemies. He made the poor and disenfranchised a priority for Catholics. He once said, "I am attracted to two sides at once because the cross always divides."

Many consider Paul "the first modern pope" (Hebblethwaite 1993). Others have seen him as Catholicism's bridge to the modern world (Wolff 2002). His confessor, the blind Jesuit Father Paolo Dezza, simply said, "If Paul VI was not a saint when he was elected pope, he became one during his papacy."

In 2003 in California and 2014 in Verona, Italy, two miracles were attributed to the intercession of Blessed Paul VI, both involving unexplained cures of unborn babies. On October 14, 2018 in Rome, Giovanni Battista Montini was canonized by Pope Francis, joining the communion of saints. His feast day is May 29, the day of his ordination to the priesthood.

He once said, "Perhaps the Lord has called me and preserved me for this service, not because I am particularly fit for it, or so that I can govern and rescue the Church from her present difficulties, but so that I can suffer something for the Church, and in that way it will be clear that Christ, and no other, is her guide and savior."

Collect From the Missal of the Sovereign Military Order of Malta[2]

Almighty ever-living God, who chose blessed Paul VI to preside over your whole people and benefit them by word and example, keep safe, we pray, by his intercession, the shepherds of your Church along with the flocks entrusted to their care, and direct them in the way of eternal salvation. Through our Lord Jesus Christ, your Son, who lives and reigns with you in the unity of the Holy Spirit, one God, for ever and ever. Amen.

---

[2] This collect commemorates Pope St. Paul VI's beatification. As of the date of this book's publication, the collect to be used after his canonization has not yet been approved by the Vatican.

18

Servant of God Andrew Bertie

1929–2008

Servant of God Andrew Willoughby Ninian Bertie, the seventy-eighth grand master of the Sovereign Military Order of Malta, was born in London in 1929. He entered the order in 1956 and was elected grand master on April 18, 1988. He died in Rome on February 7, 2008.

Andrew Bertie was born on May 15, 1929. His father, Sir James Willoughby Bertie (1901–1966), and his mother, Lady Jean Crichton-Stuart, daughter of the fourth Marquess of Bute, were married on June 12, 1928. Both came from well-known British aristocratic families. Sir James, the youngest son of the seventh Earl of Abington, was a lieutenant commander in the Royal Navy, serving in both the First (1914–1919) and Second (1939–1945) World Wars.

The Willoughby line of the family was ennobled in 1313 when King Edward II made Robert de Willoughby the first Baron of Willoughby. The Berties were also one of the most ancient lineages in England. Andrew's paternal grandfather was Montagu Arthur Bertie (1836–1928), seventh Earl of

Abington, a title that was created in 1682 for James Bertie, the fifth Baron Norreys of Rycote. Through his mother, Andrew was related to the Scottish royal family, the Stuarts. He was also a distant cousin of Queen Elizabeth II.

As might be expected, Andrew was given a typical education for English Catholic aristocrats. After Catholic primary school, he attended the well-known Catholic boarding school, Ampleforth College, operated by the Benedictines. By all accounts, Andrew was a good student with an obvious facility for languages. Later in life, he referred often to Benedictine spirituality as a model, and he viewed it as an important element of the spirituality of the Order of Malta.

At the conclusion of his secondary school education, Andrew enlisted in the Royal Scots Guards, serving from 1948 to 1950. He then attended Oxford University (Christ Church) where in 1954 he earned his bachelor's degree in modern history followed by a master's degree in 1957. He also pursued further studies at London University's School of Oriental and African Studies. He ultimately achieved fluency in five languages and competency in many others, including Sanskrit and Tibetan.

In 1956, Andrew entered the Order of Malta as a knight of honor and devotion. It did not take very long for him to find himself volunteering to alleviate suffering in the midst of a major European crisis. In that same year, Hungarians rose up in rebellion against Soviet communist domination of their country. After a brief period of unexpected initial success by the insurgents, the Soviet military crushed the revolt, and thousands of Hungarians fled the country. Refugee camps were established along the Austrian side of the

Austro-Hungarian border, and Bertie volunteered to travel to the camps to assist in caring for the displaced Hungarians.

As a young man, Andrew held several positions as he sought to decide on a profession. He was, in turn, a financial journalist and a pharmaceutical salesman before settling on teaching as a career. His first position in education was as an assistant master at London's St. Philip's School in Kensington, a small Catholic school founded by the Oratorians in 1934 for boys from seven to thirteen years old. Andrew began to realize that he was never happier than when around youngsters and that in teaching he had found his secular calling. He soon moved on to Worth School, a preparatory school attached to the Benedictine Worth Abbey in West Sussex. He remained there teaching languages for twenty-three years.

Andrew found a home at Worth among the Benedictines and the students. He was both remembered and beloved by his students. Upon hearing that the Vatican had proclaimed him a servant of God, a first step to possible sainthood, the Worth alumni newsletter, in a warm tribute to Bertie, observed that he was certainly "zany and eccentric and with no aura of holiness." Father Stephan Ortiger, a Benedictine faculty colleague of Andrew's said, "He didn't have an aura of holiness, not because he wasn't holy but because he would rather die than exude an aura of holiness." His former students admired him as "very humble and very focused [and] down-to-earth" despite "all the lofty titles and blue blood" (Pentin 2013).

Bertie's eccentricity is fondly mentioned by students and friends who have told various stories attesting to the accuracy of this description. Father Ortiger relates how, crossing the campus on the way to breakfast, Andrew would loudly sing out the Muslim call to prayer, Allahu Akbar. "No other Roman Catholic school in England . . . could boast this distinctive feature," recalled Father Ortiger, who added, "He was deliberately zany, deliberately eccentric."

At Worth, Bertie became known for a tendency to look out for the underdog and the marginalized. He was generous, humble, and joyful, offering hospitality to all and displaying a particular concern for the poor. In 1960, he established a program at the school that brought students to Lourdes on the annual Order of Malta pilgrimage. The students worked side-by-side with other Order of Malta volunteers. His faithful participation in the pilgrimage underscored his intense devotion to the Blessed Mother and his care for the sick and poor, sentiments Bertie tried to engender in his students through the experience of Lourdes.

Those who knew him best during these years said that he seemed "in the world, but not of the world." He was not bound to the trappings of his social status, nor was he enamored with material goods. Some former students speculated that he had but two suits, which he alternated wearing. When he would visit his parents' home in Malta on holiday, he apparently drove an old rusty Fiat and taught judo to Maltese youngsters. (He was a black belt.) Friends from his Worth years viewed him as a person who strove to reach and impart the "highest ideals." They greeted Bertie's designation as servant of God as natural and deserving, even if "he himself would have been both amused and surprised" (Pentin 2013).

In 1968, Bertie became a knight of obedience, and nine years later, in 1977, he professed his first (temporary) vows of poverty, chastity, and obedience as a knight of justice. In 1981, he made his final (perpetual) vows. Later that same year, he joined the Sovereign Council, the ruling body of the order consisting of nine members, an important step in obtaining the experience necessary for a future grand master. This is not to say that this was at all on Frá Andrew's mind. He remained true to his character: humble, patient, and unassuming, without guile or personal ambition, focused on serving the poor. Still, whether or not Frá Andrew displayed any interest in being grand master hardly matters. The fact remained that he was clearly a leading candidate. He possessed the requisite nobiliary requirements, he was well-liked throughout the order, and he was relatively young at the age of fifty-two when he took a seat on the Sovereign Council.

When Frá Andrew entered the order in 1956, it was facing a major crisis. Its leadership was fending off a serious attempt by Cardinal Nicola Canali and his Vatican allies to take control of the order. In 1951, Grand Master Ludovico, Prince Chigi Albani della Rovere, died, and Pope Pius XII, who was heavily influenced by Canali, refused to allow the order to elect a new grand master. This set off a seven-year battle, which saw the Canali camp use a call for reform of the order as a stalking horse for its power grab.

The struggle for the order ended only when Cardinal Angelo Roncalli ascended to the throne of St. Peter as Pope John XXIII. Cardinal Canali fell out of favor, and the order was charged to review its constitutions without undue outside interference. In 1961, Pope John approved the new constitutions, including a reaffirmation of all the historical prerogatives granted to the professed, and gave permission to elect a new grand master. In 1962, after eleven years without a grand master, Frá Angelo de Mojana di Cologna was chosen as the seventy-seventh head of the order.

When Grand Master Angelo de Mojana died in 1988, Frá Andrew had been in the order for thirty-two years, twenty-six of which were during Frá Angelo's reign. He had entered the order when it was engaged in its struggle with Canali—no doubt an unforgettable experience, even when viewed from a distance. He had worked on a myriad of ministries for the youth, the poor, and the sick. At the time of Frá Angelo's passing, he was a seasoned professed knight of justice, former regent of the English Sub-Priory, and a member of the Sovereign Council. On April 8, 1988, Frá Andrew Willoughby Bertie was elected the seventy-eighth grand master, the first Englishman chosen to lead the Knights of St. John in its nine-hundred-year history.

Although shy and reserved, the new grand master set about successfully modernizing elements of the order. He summoned a council on future strategies in 1988 to achieve consensus on the way forward for the ancient order. Many of the reforms and advances that occurred under Grand Master Bertie flowed from the conclusions of this strategic review.

Under Frá Andrew, national associations were asked to share more systematic financial and operating information with the Grand Magistry. He insisted that membership in the order not be seen as an honorific achievement. Rather, it should be regarded as a commitment to actual hands-on work with the poor and sick. He led by example each year at the Lourdes pilgrimage when the order brought thousands of sick to the Marian shrine and by countless other acts of service to his lords, the sick and the poor. Under his patronage, the annual Lourdes pilgrimage grew into a major international religious event.

In government, he worked successfully to expand the number of countries with which the order had diplomatic recognition. He saw the sovereignty of the order as an important tool to open doors and to provide support for the order's considerable humanitarian aid throughout the world. During his reign, the number of countries with which the order exchanged ambassadors rose from forty-nine to one hundred, and its global relief aid, through Malteser, grew exponentially. Frá Andrew emphasized the need for a more professional diplomatic corps to facilitate and look after the order's growing international presence. He took measures to broaden the appeal of the order and to enhance the role of women in its works.

Before he became grand master, Frá Andrew lived his religious life much as knights of justice had since at least the sixteenth century: living on his own, financially and otherwise responsible for himself, witnessing Christ at his workplace, and finding community in the priory and in works of the order. He understood the value of the order's specific way of religious life, and he was able to pursue his path to holiness through its means. As such, Frá Andrew worked assiduously to increase the number of professed, recognizing their critical role in ensuring both the religious and sovereign natures of the order.

When he took the helm, the number of professed knights of justice had been steadily declining since the post-World War II years. During this time, it was not sufficient to discern a vocation to pursue a religious life as a knight of justice. The religious of the Order of Malta were required to meet a certain standard of nobility. The new grand master decided to drop the nobiliary requirements for knights of justice, and the number of professed slowly began to trend upward, reaching a relatively strong number of sixty-six under his successor, Frá Matthew Festig. Frá Matthew continued to carry out Frá Andrew's emphasis on fostering vocations to the order's traditional, yet unique, form of religious life. Frá Andrew's example and efforts on behalf of the professed resulted in the entrance of a sufficient number of knights of justice to enable the re-founding of the English Grand Priory in 1993 and the establishment of two sub-priories in the United States.

Frá Andrew was a cultured and educated man with an encyclopedic mind and irrepressible intellect. Frá James Michael von Strobel, a professed knight who worked with the grand master during the constitutional reform of 1996 and knew him well, said of Frá Andrew: "He was approachable and understanding of human foibles, but he did not suffer fools well. He was a true gentleman of the old school, with impeccable manners and impeccable taste in clothes. . . . Let there be no doubt, he was most definitely eccentric. But he was authentic. . . . He enjoyed evenings at the Magistral Palace when after supper he and those living there (and sometimes guests) would join him for a smoke and post-prandial libation.

He smoked Gauloises almost continually. . . . Conversations were always interesting and instructive."

Behind all the activity and growth of the 1990s and early 2000s stood Frá Andrew, a quiet, unassuming, and cultured leader. At the opening of Bertie's cause for sainthood, Cardinal Agostino Vallini, vicar general of the Diocese of Rome, said that Frá Andrew's obvious serenity was "a sign of the continual taming of his interior life, developed through prayer and acts of charity." Frá James-Michael echoed these sentiments when he wrote, "By his profound spiritual and human virtues . . . Frá Andrew showed signs of heroic virtue. . . . He had no shortage of fortitude, stability, humility, and he displayed a profound sense of service to others."

In a brief but heartfelt remembrance of the grand master, Monsignor Giovanni Scarabelli, a professed chaplain, related how he was struck by the image of Frá Andrew deep in prayer, oblivious to his surroundings (Studi Melintensi, XXVI 2018). Others, like Frá James Michael, commented on Frá Andrew's intensity of prayer after the reception of the Eucharist. Many Lourdes pilgrims witnessed this as well, as Scarabelli notes: "On his spirituality, it would suffice to make mention of his concentration, so visible, when he entered into prayer. He was estranged from the surrounding environment, absorbed and subsumed in an interior dialogue that did not allow any room for distractions. A number of photographs of him at the Grotto in Lourdes, for example, are documentation enough" (Scarabelli 2018).

On February 7, 2008 in Rome, the seventy-eighth grand master of the Order of Malta, after a brief but painful illness, succumbed to cancer. His was a legacy of intense prayer life and unfailing service. His profound spirituality nurtured his care for the poor and sick and inspired his dedication to spreading Christ's love to the world through the Order of Malta.

In February 2013, the authorities of the Diocese of Rome made a formal request to the Vatican to initiate the procedure for Frá Andrew's beatification. Two years later, the Vatican approved the opening of the cause for his canonization. This approval was marked with a Mass and ceremony at St. John Lateran Basilica on February 20, 2015, only the second time that the storied church had witnessed an official opening of the canonization process. The first was that of St. John Paul II in 2005.

Frá Andrew Bertie was born in privilege with a social status that is much admired and envied by many people around the world, yet his life developed in most unexpected ways. Humble, kind, and caring, he ultimately discovered his own path to holiness through the Order of Malta. His life included innumerable good works on behalf of the sick, the orphaned, and the needy. These were not, however, simply "gestures of human solidarity." Rather, as Cardinal Vallini said, these were acts nurtured by the depth of his intimate friendship with God. They were an integral part of his "hymn of love and constant praise to the Lord" (Vallini 2015). They demonstrated that, in the end, Frá Andrew Bertie's life was one of heroic virtue that blessed the Order of Malta and all who knew him.

Conclusion

All saints speak to the people of their times. Some are the focus of local prayer cults, while others appeal to a wider audience. Some are patrons of professions, guilds, towns, and nations, while others are intercessors for specific maladies, like throat ailments, cancer, or multiple sclerosis. Some have an intensive following for a brief period, while others are rediscovered by one generation after another, still relevant centuries after the end of their lives on earth. The saints speak to the people of their times because the saints themselves are men and women of those same times. The saints are also human beings with all their frailties, weaknesses, and imperfections who, in the words of Blessed Miriam Teresa Demjanovich, SC, "did but one thing—the will of God. But they did it with all their might" (Geis 1957).

In a time in history, the Middle Ages, when miracles made the saint, it is not difficult to see why everyday men and women felt that sainthood was beyond their reach. They stood in awe of the miracle worker whose tomb became a place of healing. They shrank away, out of fear or respect, from the saint who bore the stigmata or levitated during Mass or gazed into their hearts and saw their future. They could recognize and acclaim the saints living among them, but it never occurred to them that they could be one of them. For all practical purposes, the call to holiness was for someone very special, but for someone else.

This is one of the reasons why the historical truth surrounding the saints, even an approximation of that truth, is critically important. In many instances, the contrived stories and false narratives only serve to make the saint less human, more unapproachable, and strangely unfamiliar. Rather than encouraging normal men and women to achieve personal holiness, the saints of the exaggerated hagiographies become examples too difficult to follow or models too foreign to imitate.

This is not to say that the saints were not exceptional human beings. They most assuredly were, and in many ways: the intensity of their prayer lives, their complete submission to the will of God, their ability to recognize contemporary demands of social justice, and their extraordinary care for the poor. By and large, these are the exceptional characteristics found in the holy men and women of the Church, characteristics that bear imitation, not unnecessary exaggeration. In all of this, it is important to note that the saints of the Order of Malta, like all saints, were not holy because they performed miracles. Rather, they could perform miracles because they were holy.

Perhaps the enduring popularity of the saints, despite the problems associated with medieval hagiography, speaks to the visceral relevance that they have to human nature. It is somehow comforting to know that the saints were friends, neighbors, colleagues, and relatives of average, everyday people. Like everyday people, the saints had to eat to survive, work to live, sin to be forgiven, and suffer illness to die. The order's saints of the modern age are perhaps the best examples of this familiarity that should engender in everyone the confidence that holiness is within their grasp.

Take, for example, Pope St. Paul VI. Where was his heroic virtue if not in his patient love for all segments of the Church at a time when traditionalists were equating progressives with Satan and progressives demanding sanctions against traditionalists? Paul's contemporaries saw him as weak and indecisive, and they believed that the reforms of Vatican II were tearing the Church asunder, while Paul did nothing. They could not see that, in part, his holiness was in his refusal to demonize either his critics or the opponents of the Vatican II reforms, and in his unshakable faith that ultimately God would not allow the destruction of his Church. His humble, patient, and steady implementation of the reforms set free the spirit of Vatican II and transformed the Church.

Blessed Clemens von Galen is not celebrated for miracle working but rather for the courage he displayed in speaking truth to the diabolical at great risk to his own life. This is not to say that von Galen was reckless. In fact, he walked a fine line between patriotism to his homeland and the obligation to speak out against the immorality, racism, and atheism of the Nazi regime. Many of his fellow bishops, including the primate of Germany, did not raise their voices. When heroic virtue summoned them to sainthood, they did not hear the call. Almost alone among his fellow German prelates, von Galen did.

The English martyrs displayed their imperfect human natures for all to see. They argued over sinecures and appointments within the order. They fought duels and were even imprisoned for violence. In sum, they were imperfect but essentially good men, as one might expect of many knights in the sixteenth-century Order of St. John. Yet when imprisoned by Henry VIII, tortured mercilessly and pressed to renounce their faith, they did not act like so many others. Somehow, they each found the courage to stand fast in their faith and accept the deadly consequences of their refusals. This is an example of heroic virtue.

Within the Church, the saints have traditionally served as examples of how to live a Christian life, and the saints of the Order of Malta provide their own guideposts to this goal. Its holy men and women often displayed an exceptional love for the poor—whether it was St. Ugo Canefri and his hospital in Genoa or St. Paul VI and the preferential option for the poor. They taught courage, as befits saints of a military order—whether it was Blessed David Gonson as he awaited his gruesome execution or Blessed Vilmos Apor confronting Soviet soldiers. They encouraged humility among the powerful—whether it was Blessed Charles of Austria, the last emperor of the Habsburg line, or St. Nuno Alvarez Pereira, the hero of Portuguese independence. They underscored the value of prayer—whether it was St. Fleur levitating while deep in contemplation or the image of Frá Andrew Bertie praying at the Grotto in Lourdes.

For a nine-hundred-year-old religious order, the Order of Malta does not have a great number of saints and blessed. The Jesuits, founded in 1540, have a total of fifty-three canonized saints alone, and the Dominican litany of its saints and blessed includes fifty-eight men and women. There are some explanations for these disparities, which come down to the systemic difference between the religious military Order of Malta and other religious orders.

For one, the military aspect of the order, which was a major focus of its activities from the mid-twelfth to eighteenth century, made the leadership reluctant to single out as martyrs individual knights or soldiers fallen on the battlefield. In a certain way, it may have been that all members of the order who gave their lives in battle for the Faith were considered as martyrs and therefore saints. It may also be, as some historians have speculated, that the order found it difficult to choose which fallen knights to promote as saintly martyrs and which to pass over without hurting morale and military discipline. In any case, it is clear that throughout its history, the order made very little effort to promote the cause of any of its saints and blessed with the on-going exception of Frá Andrew Bertie.

The order has not engaged in military activity since 1798 and the loss of Malta to Napoleon. Instead, in these last two hundred years, it has concentrated on developing its Hospitaller function, transforming it into a world-class, global Catholic relief organization sponsoring thousands of charitable programs and initiatives. Yet, the order remains a religious congregation with professed knights who take the evangelical vows of poverty, chastity, and obedience. Apart from these vowed religious, the order provides a means of personal sanctification for over thirteen thousand laymen and laywomen who are knights and dames. Perhaps now, with its membership focused entirely on caring for the poor and sick, more contemporary saints, like Frá Andrew, will arise from the ranks of the order to continue the line of holy Hospitaller men and women into the next millennium.

Appendix 1

Feast Days of the Saints and Blessed of the Order

January

   3   Blessed Garcia Martinez

March

  22   Blessed Clemens August von Galen

April

   1   St. Nuno Alvarez Pereira

May

  18   Blessed Gerard Mecatti

  23   Blessed Vilmos Apor

  29   Pope St. Paul VI

  28   St. Ubaldesca

June

  12   St. Fleur of Beaulieu

  19   Blessed Gerland

  24   Nativity of St. John the Baptist, Patron of the Order of Malta

July

   1   St. Nicasius

   8   Blessed Adrian Fortescue

12   Blessed David Gunston

14   St. Toscana

August

30   Blessed Alfredo Ildefonso Schuster

September

8   Our Lady of Philermo, Patroness of the Order

October

5   Blessed Peter Pattarini

8   St. Ugo Canefri

11   Pope St. John XXIII

13   Blessed Gerard, Founder

21   Blessed Charles of Austria

November

19   All the Saints of the Order

December

2   The Blessed Virgin Mary, Cause of Our Joy

Appendix 2

Litany of the Saints and Blessed of the Order of Malta

Lord have mercy, Lord have mercy.
Christ have mercy, Christ have mercy.
Lord have mercy, Lord have mercy.
Christ hear us, Christ graciously hear us.

God, our Father in heaven, Have mercy on us.
God, the Son, Redeemer of the world, Have mercy on us.
God, the Holy Spirit, Have mercy on us.
Holy Trinity, one God, Have mercy on us.

Holy Mary, Mother of our Lord and Savior Jesus Christ, Pray for us.
Holy Virgin of Philermos, Pray for us.
Blessed Virgin Mary, Cause of Our Joy and Our Lady of Liesse, Pray for us.
Holy Father, Blessed Frá Gerard, Pray for us.
Saint Ubaldesca, Virgin, Pray for us.
Saint Fleur of Beaulieu, Virgin, Pray for us.
Saint Nicasius, Martyr, Pray for us.
Saint Toscana, Religious, Pray for us.

Saint Hugh, Religious, Pray for us.
Saint Nuno Alvares Pereira, Lay Brother, Pray for us.
Saint John XXIII, Pope, Pray for us.
St. Paul VI, Pope, Pray for us.

All you Saints of the Order of Malta, Pray for us.

Blessed Clemens August Cardinal von Galen, Bishop, Pray for us.
Blessed Gerard Mecatti of Villamagna, Religious, Pray for us.
Blessed Vilmos Apor, Bishop and Martyr, Pray for us.
Blessed Gerland, Religious, Pray for us.
Blessed Adrian Forescue, Martyr, Pray for us.
Blessed David Gunston, Martyr, Pray for us.
Blessed Alfredo Ildefonso Schuster, Bishop, Pray for us.
Blessed Peter Pattarini, Prior, Pray for us.
Blessed Emperor Charles of Austria, Pray for us.
All you Blessed of the Order of Malta, Pray for us.

Father of our Lord and Savior Jesus Christ, though we are sinners, you have called us to be Christ's companions and to live out our lives serving the poor and sick and defending the Holy Roman Catholic Faith. Bring to completion in us the work that You began in Blessed Frá Gerard and his followers through the centuries. Place us with Your Son and gather us under the Cross of Malta to serve Him alone and His Church. We ask this through Christ our Lord. Amen.

Frá Richard J. Wolff

References

Artuino, Fabio. 2012. Beato Pietro di Imola, Cavalliere di Malta. Santiebeati.it.

Bell, Rudolph M. 1985. *Holy Anorexia*. Chicago: University of Chicago Press.

Boeselager, Philipp von. 2009. *Valkyrie: The Story of the Plot to Kill Hitler By Its Last Member*. New York: Alfred A. Knopf.

Bogle, James and Joanna. 1993. *A Heart for Europe*. Herefordshire: Gracewing.

Brook-Shepherd, Gordan. 1968. *The Last Habsburg*. New York: Weybright and Talley.

Brunell,Clovis. 1946. "Vida e miracles de sancta Flor." Analeccta Bollandiana, 64.

Cahill, Thomas. 2002. *Pope John XXIII*. New York: Viking.

Capuzza, Vittorio. 2018. *Fra`Andrew Bertie. The First Servant of God Grand Master of the Sovereign Military Order of Malta*. Velar.

Cavallari, V. 1974-75. "Considerazioni e congetture sui tempi di Santa Toscana. Studi Storici Veronesi Luigi Simeoni.

Cunningham, Lawrence S. 2005. *A Brief History of the Saints*. Malden, MA: Blackwell.

Demurger, Alain. 2005. *Caballeros de Cristo: hospitalarios, teutonicos, y demas ordenes militares en la edad media (siglos XI a XVI)*. Granada: Universidad de Granada.

Ebejer, Matthias. 2017. "'Sanctify yourselves and be holy': Hospitallers and their Counter-Reformation Saints." Journal of Baroque Studies vol. 2.

Editors, June 2020. "Nuno Alvares Pereira: Portuguese Military Leader," Encyclopedia Britannica.

Epstein, Steven. 1996. *Genoa and the Genoese, 958-1528*. Chapel Hill: University of North Carolina Press.

Geis, Mary Zita. 1957. *Sister Miriam Teresa Demjanovich, SC (1901-1927)*. New York: Benziger Brothers.

Gori, Annarita. 2010. "Festa da Patria: Nuno Alvares Pereira: Eroi e Santo." Republicas Ler Historia, v. 59.

Griech-Polelle, Beth A. 2002. *Bishop von Galen: German Catholicism and National Socialism*. New Haven & London: Yale University Press.

Hebblethwaite, Peter. 1993. *Paul VI, The First Modern Pope*. New York: Paulist Press.

Heubsch, Bill. 2014. *The Spiritual Wisdom of St. John XXIII*. New York: Paulist Press.

Krotzl, Christian. 2012. "How to Choose a Saint? On Propagation, Advice, and Decision-making in Medieval Communities." In *Hagiography and Popular Cultures*, edited by Paolo Golinelli. Bologna: CLUEB.

L'Hermite-Leclercq, Paulette. 2006. "Fleur de Beaulieu (d. 1347), Saint of the Hospital of St. John of Jerusalem," in Anthony Luttrell and Helen J. Nicholson, *Hospitaller Women in the Middle Ages*.

London: Ashgate Publishing Company.

Leal, Ernesto Castro. 2010. *Nuno Alvares: Simbol e Mito nos Seculos XIX e XX*. Lusitania Sacra.

Leo Valiani. 1973. *The End of Austria-Hungary*. New York: Alfred A. Knopf.

Licence, Tom. 2005. "The Templars and the Hospitallers, Christ and the Saints," in Benjamin Z. Kedar and Jonathan Riley-Smith, eds. *The Crusades* vol. 4, London: Ashgate.

Luttrell, Anthony and Helen J. Nicholson, eds. 2006. *Hospitaller Women in the Middle Ages*. London: Ashgate.

Maalouf, Jean. 2008. *Pope John XXIII, Essential Writings*. New York: Orbis Books.

Marshall, Peter and Geoffry Scott, eds. 2016. *Catholic Gentry in English Society*. New York: Routledge.

Monteiro, Joao Gouveia. 2017. *Nuno Alvares Pereira, Guerrerio, Senhor Feudal, Santo: os Tres Rostros do Condestavel*. Lisbon: Manuscrito Editora.

Morris, John. 1887. *The Venerable Sir Adrian Fortescue, Knight of the Bath, Knight of St. John, Martyr*. London: Burns and Oates.

Morton, Nicholas. 2017. "Why did some military orders become great institutions while others remained small scale?" In *The Service of Monuments*, eds. Janusz Hochleitner and Karol Polejowski. Marlbork.

Nemeth, Laszlo Imre. 2011. *Beato Vilmos Apor: Vescovo e Martire nella Tragedia del XX secolo*. Gorle, Bg.: Editrice Velar.

Nicholson, Helen J. 1990. "Images of the Military Orders, 1128-1291: Spiritual, Secular, Romantic." (Ph.D. Thesis: University of Leicester.

Nicholson, Helen. 1995. *Templars, Hospitallers and Teutonic Knights: Images of the Military Orders, 1128-1291.* Leicester University Press.

Nicholson, Helen J. 1999. "Knights of Christ? The Military Orders in the Eyes of their Contemporaries," On-Line Reference Book for Medieval Studies.

Nicholson, Helen J. 2001. *The Knights Hospitaller.* Woodridge, UK: The Boydell Press.

Nicholson, Helen J. 2010. "The Role of Women in the Military Orders," Militiae Christi: Handelingen van de Vereniging voor de Studie over de Tempeliers en de Hospitaalridders vzw, year 1.

Nicholson, Helen J. 2014. "Martyrum collegio sociandus haberet: Depictions of the Military Orders' Martyrs in the Holy Land, 1187-1291." In *Crusading and Warfare in the Middle Ages*, eds. Simon John and Nicholas Morton. Farnham: Ashgate.

Nicholson, Helen J. 2018. "Memory and the Military Orders: an Overview," *Entre Deuse e o Rei: O Mundo das Ordens Militares*, ed. Isabel Cristina Ferreira Fernandes.

Nobili, Elena. 2015. *Ildefonso Schuster e il rinnovamento cattolico (1880 – 1929).* Milano: Guerini, 5th edition.

O'Driscoll, David. 1993. *Martyr of Service and Charity: The Life of Baron Vilmos Apor.* London: Catholic Truth Society.

Pentin, Edward. 2013. "Fra'Andrew Bertie." Worth Society (January 24).

Persoglio, Vincenzo. 1878. *Sant'Ugo e la Commenda di San Giovanni de Pre'*. Genoa: Tipo Aricivescovile. Sant'Ugo Canefri da Genova su santiebeati.it

Perta, Giuseppe. 2015. "A Crusader without a sword: the sources relating to the Blessed Gerard." In *Life and Religion in the Middle Ages*, ed. Flocel Sabate. Cambridge: Cambridge Scholars Publishing.

Riley-Smith, Jonathan. 2010. *Templars and Hospitallers as Professed Religious in the Holy Land*. Notre Dame, Indiana: University of Notre Dame Press.

Rumi, Giorgio and Angelo Majo,. 1996. *Il Cardinal Schuster e il suo tempo*. Milano: Massimo-NED.

Scarabelli, Giovanni. 2018. "Dieci anni dalla morte del Servo di Dio fra` Andrew Bertie." Studi Melitensi XXVI.

Sire, H. J. A. 1994. *The Knights of Malta*. New Haven: Yale University Press.

Smith, Patrick. 1943. *The Bishop of Munster and the Nazis: The Documents in the Case*. London: Burns Oates.

Sollinas, Alberto di. 2006. *Annuario no. 13 del Comitato Beneficio di Santa Toscana*. Verona.

The Morgan Library and Museum. *Vita Christi (Scenes from the Life of Christ and the Life of Blessed Gerard of Villamagna)*. MS M.643. Firenze: c.1320.

Utrecht, Daniel. 2016. *The Lion of Munster: The Bishop Who Roared Against the Nazis*. Charlotte, North Carolina: TAN Books.

Vallini, Agosto Cardinale. 2015. "Sessione Pubblica di

Apertura dell'Inchiesta Diocesana per la Causa di Beatificazione e Canonizzazione del Servo di Dio Fra` Andrew Bertie." Unpublished Remarks (February 20).

Venuti, Vincenzo. 1762. *Della esistenza, professione e culto di S. Nicasius Martire: Discorso storico-critico.* Palermo: Stampa dei Ss. Apostoli.

Whatmore, L. E. 1949. *The Westminster Cathedral Chronicle*, "Sir David Gunston, Knight of Malta."

Wilson, Mary Leonora, ed. 2018. *Wisdom from Pope Paul VI.* New York: Paulist Press.

Wolff, Richard J. 1985. "Giovanni Battista Montini and Italian Politics: the Early Life of Pope Paul VI 1897-1933." The Catholic Historical Review 81, no. 2 (April).

Wolff, Richard J. 1990. *Between Pope and Duce: Catholic Students in Fascist Italy.* New York: Peter Lang.

Wolff, Richard J. 2002. "Pope Paul VI: Catholicism's Bridge to the Modern World." In Frank J. Coppa ed. *The Great Popes Through History.* New York: Greenwood Press.

Wolff, Richard J. and Jorg K. Hoensch. eds. 1987. *Catholics, the State and the European Radical Right.* Boulder CO: Atlantic Press.

Zaccagnini, Gabriele. 1995. *Ubaldesca, una santa laica nella Pisa dei secoli XII-XIII.* Pisa: Edizione ETC.